Happier Far

CRUX
THE GEORGIA SERIES IN LITERARY NONFICTION

Happier Far

ESSAYS

DIANE MEHTA

The University of Georgia Press
ATHENS

Published by the University of Georgia Press
Athens, Georgia 30602
www.ugapress.org

Designed by Rebecca A. Norton
Set in 10.5 / 14 Minion Pro
Printed and bound by Sheridan Books, Inc.
The paper in this book meets the guidelines for permanence and durability of the Committee on Production Guidelines for Book Longevity of the Council on Library Resources.

Most University of Georgia Press titles are available from popular e-book vendors.

Printed in the United States of America
25 26 27 28 29 P 5 4 3 2 1

Library of Congress Cataloging-in-Publication Data
Names: Mehta, Diane, author.
Title: Happier far : essays / Diane Mehta.
Description: Athens : The University of Georgia Press, 2025. |
Series: Crux: the Georgia Series of Literary Nonfiction
Identifiers: LCCN 2024035420 | ISBN 9780820373287 (paperback) |
ISBN 9780820373294 (epub) | ISBN 9780820373300 (pdf)
Subjects: LCSH: Mehta, Diane. |
Authors, American—21st century—Biography. |
LCGFT: Autobiographies. | Essays.
Classification: LCC PS3613.E4257 Z46 2025 |
DDC 818/.609 [B]—dc23/eng/20240823
LC record available at https://lccn.loc.gov/2024035420

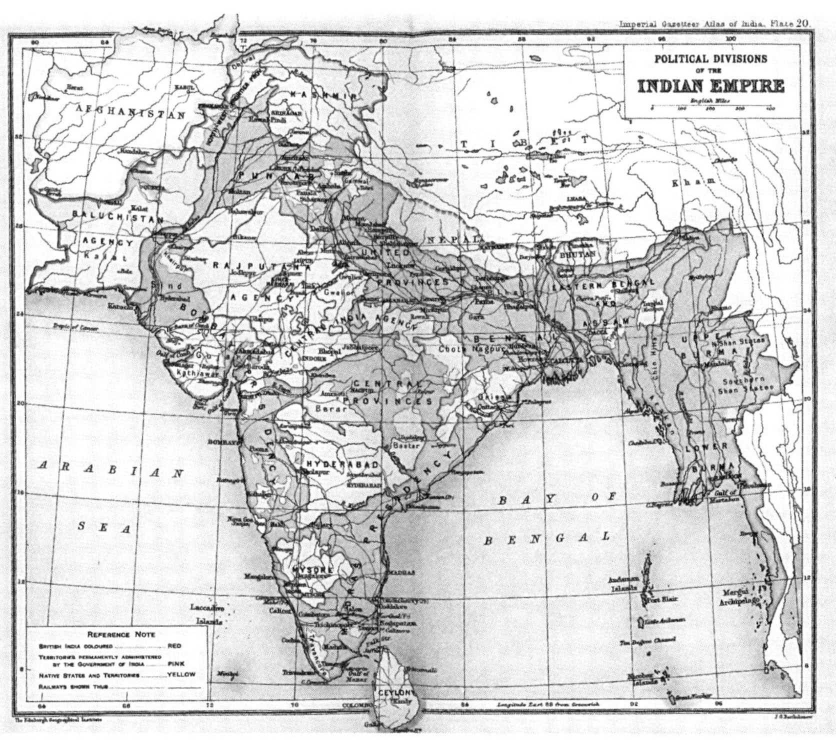

The British Indian Empire, 1909, from *The Imperial Gazetteer of India.*

For Carole A. Leonard and Dilip J. Mehta

In five goddam minutes I am going to get my act together.

Art Is Everything: A Novel
Yxta Maya Murray

In the end, there were five minutes left to live, no more. He swore that these five minutes to him seemed a countless time, an endless wealth; he saw himself live a thousand lifetimes, and there was little point in worrying about his last moments, so he planned them out instead: he gave himself two minutes to say goodbye to his comrades, two more to think one last time about himself, and a final moment to look around himself for the last time.

The Idiot
Fyodor Dostoevsky

Contents

Part I

Unreal History of My Childhood

Documents

The birth certificate that documents my entry into the world is the first of many documents that explain my life, but when I look at it, things go wrong immediately. My birth certificate says I am Diane Sarah Mehta, daughter of Carole A. Leonard and Dilip J. Mehta. I was born in a hospital in Frankfurt am Main on May 12, 1966. The tiny pink wristband with a snap button identifies me as ♀, 3,000 grams (6.6 pounds) and 50 centimeters (19.6 inches) long.

This announcement says I was born, but doesn't specify if I was reborn, a viable option for the daughter of an Indian Jain, who, if he were practicing, might believe in rebirth and nirvana. It doesn't say what kind of Jewish household my mother will keep, or whether I was expected to believe in a God who is, in the traditional sense of the word, a maker. It doesn't say how dangerous my birth was, but I know that it was risky for my mother to have children. The birth certificate tells me nothing about what transpired in the four days I was in the hospital with my mother. It doesn't express the May 12 Frankfurt weather, a lovely 25.5 degrees Celsius at 7:00 p.m., or the angle of Earth in regard to the moon, or how much the moon pulled at the tide, and it makes no reference to my time of birth. Instead of describing the colors in rotation across the world that night, there is a galaxy of white space between the words.

My mother gave birth to me alone, in a foreign country, an omen of lonelinesses to come. Because my mother is dead, those days will always be a mystery. She told me once that she didn't remember the birth, and that the German nurses were mean and refused to help her go to the toilet or get onto the delivery table. I imagine a steel table similar to those in police procedural thrillers, washed clean of victims who were dissected there, as the vehicle for my entry into life. For a Jewish American woman living in postwar Germany, the nurses' refusal to help her bring my blood-and-bones being into being must have felt like an absence of compassion and a pathological condition of German society, which had tuned itself out to the normal preindustrial processing of empathy. I am certain that my mother hated every moment of my birth, and I imagine it felt like a sanatorium instead of a place where you deliver an unfettered creature into kaleidoscopic new life.

Those days in the hospital are better served by myth, so I create an alternate narrative, because the relationship is mine to shape now. My mother had a view southeast over rooftops that maintained the same stern facade as the woeful labor and delivery nurses who spent their lives listening to women screaming. For them, pain had lost its context. But they believed that fresh air aided the constitution, so they left the windows open. We smelled diesel from engines driving boats along the river. It was spring, and laughter floated about in the soprano voices of young women looking for husbands or escaping them. When they rolled my bassinet into the room with the other German just-borns, I learned that many of us would be shipped off to half-timbered homes along the riverbanks, and others would live above grocers, and I would live in a flat. I discovered that I would be bottle-fed. When I complained to my mother about missing out, she reminded me that I had emerged whole, with ten fingers and ten toes, and that this itself was a miracle of design, though God, we agreed, did not exist in a postwar world.

When my father showed up, he told me what to make of the world, and when he left, my mother edited his advice a little. She said never learn to sew more than a button, and don't bother getting married, but definitely have children, even if it's risky, as it is for me with my congenitally enlarged, unstable heart, because nothing lasts except your children once you place them in the world. Stick with me, she said.

My father helps me patchwork my story with facts, but much of the content is missing. Höchst am Main, where I was born, was an independent historic city on the north bank of the Main River, and became part of Frankfurt am Main in 1928. The town, a center for porcelain manufacturing, became known for Hoechst AG, a chemical-dye manufacturer that evolved into the pharmaceutical company where my father worked and the subject of an exhaustive study by the historian Stephan H. Lindner, who documented Hoechst's complicity during the Third Reich. (My father took the job nineteen years after the fall of the Third Reich.) He was a minority and a citizen of India, and husband to a minority Jewish American wife, and he was the rising star at this company that had once produced half the Zyklon B for the death camps in Germany. My father told Hoechst that he wanted to launch clinical research in India instead of Europe; it had never been done, yet they agreed. He was thirty-three.

But when he arrived with my mother at the hospital, the attendants shooed him away at the door, and no amount of arguing could convince them to let him stay the night. My parents had arranged for a female obstetrician to deliver me, a woman with whom they had scheduled many prenatal visits, but I was swept out of the womb by the male head of obstetrics instead. My unruffled, handsome, and quietly commanding father must have been irritated at being so dismissed. He does not see himself as a discounted version of a European because he is dark-skinned. He grew up in the North Indian town of Rajkot, under colonialism, an ordinary citizen who was not allowed to frequent the same places as Europeans. He trained as a physician and traveled to America in the sixties, married a woman he loved, and helped blaze a trail developing a framework for clinical research. But whom did the German matrons see, brown knuckled, at the door?

When he returned in the morning, they told him that he had a daughter.

I send him emails, but I do not get the answer I am looking for: two thousand solar flares shot out, and purple-pink and alligator-green auroras drifted over Frankfurt for the first time, and it was recorded as an unusual incident at an impossible time of year, perhaps a UFO or a military exercise. Streets were filled with women.

All the trees turned upside-down and stuck their roots straight up—and experimented with becoming banyan trees when their roots began searching for the ground. I had planted myself here. The world would be forever mixed; now Germany had some India and more Ashkenazi Jew in it.

Because my mother is dead and my father is old, I would like to know whether she held me when I cried or left me to the nurses, and whether in those first moments she immediately loved me or whether it took a while. I didn't ask him this question. He and I both think I'm after the valuable facts. He tells me that my mother often sat with me outside, on a bench, with my sister, and that she had met another Jewish woman, named Bernstein, who was there to collect her family's property, and what stands out to him is that the Bernstein lady did not know that my mother was Jewish, because she had taken my father's surname.

My mother's surname was Leonard, airbrushed from Levine to cloak the family's Jewish identity from gentiles who might do them harm. My maternal ancestors had emigrated to the United States from Minsk, Poland, and London, as rabbis, umbrella salesmen, tailors, and wives. At first, I discounted this detail; so my mother made a Jewish friend in Germany, and they chatted on a bench. But over months of digging for information that did not yield the satisfaction I wanted, it hit me that this Bernstein woman was not just looking to gain her rightful property, as recompense, but was using the legal system to rebuild the architecture of her family's former life, before they fled Frankfurt, through their possessions. In the process of procuring the documents she needed, she was, in her tiny way, reclaiming something still intact from the jaws of an annihilating genocide, and maybe, in her commitment to retrieving what had been stolen from her family, she might reinvent that time of childhood in Frankfurt. But what pained me was what was lost in my mother's own name and her own childhood life. Excising her given name from her marriage contract opened up the possibility that she would lose track of who she was.

We allow documents to betray what is legally and emotionally ours in countless ways, and other ways in which they seal our fate.

What emotions do women feel when they get married and choose to sign their names away? Perhaps my mother enjoyed folding herself into my father by following tradition, a contract: that let her be, as John Donne said, in "A Valediction: Forbidding Mourning," "like a compass, fixed and free." He would care for her and keep her safe. The marriage had already disappointed both sets of parents: hers because she was marrying an Indian Jain instead of a white Jew, and his because he was marrying a white American woman who would keep him in America. It is not unusual to hang on to pipe dreams around heritage, genetics, color, and sect when it comes to our children, in the hope that they will carry on our tradition and our sense of self after our bodies are gone. My mother sawed away the name Leonard, chopped from Levine, but like all of us, she had only half of a name: the father, the patriarch, the money earner, the strongman. How did she feel about being "Mrs. Mehta" when strangers excised her first name?

The word "document" originates from the Latin *documentum*, which means "lesson, proof, instance, specimen," according to the *Oxford English Dictionary* (OED). This document itself embodies an experiment in truth-making. The medieval Latin word is closer to the contemporary meaning of "instrument, charter, official paper." More promising, for my purposes, is the Latin *docēre*: "to teach." How much recompense for suffering that this term ignites! What we learn, or struggle to learn or appreciate, is how to create phosphorescence from dull life. Alas, the OED marks all the usages before the eighteenth century as obsolete, which distracts from the fact that all meanings are evidentiary, even if settled usage is closer to what the OED tracks to 1728, when the word appears in Ephraim Chambers's *Cyclopædia; or, an Universal Dictionary of Arts and Sciences*: "title deed, tombstone, coin, picture." The OED has made a mistake: if you skip the thousand-year history of the Latin, you lose the thrill of *docēre*. Language is there to lose and find, but not to lose.

"Encompass worlds, but never try to encompass me," says Walt Whitman in "Song of Myself," a poem in which he left out nothing, as if to say: Do not restrict me in body or idea. Whitman, who had no truck with anyone, didn't want to be misunderstood, but I think he wasn't entirely comfortable being understood, either, because if his output were perceived as the full measure of his being, then his encompassing lists would encompass him, and he would never be free. He slashed what was intrusive by saying, "I crowd your noisiest talk by looking toward you." It is an agitated and awkward way of crushing opposition with certainty of mind. My mother, even without her surname to center her, could do this, too.

I believe my parents had intellectually slingabout ways that guaranteed they could survive in Whitmanesque worlds; I mean, they were both so meticulous about using the mind to soften the sting of the body. For my father, that meant understanding psychopharmacology, the effect of drugs on the mind in an individual body—the efficacy of a drug, and how it interacts with other drugs or with food, as measures of statistical truth. For my mother, it meant allowing abstractions to fulfill what reality is not doing. One day, when I was a teenager, my mother and I were looking at a book with reproductions of paintings. She showed me two images of an industrial English landscape and asked which I preferred. She excoriated me for preferring the prettier, realistic painting. The other had looser brushstrokes, and the buildings were blurry and textured. It was a darkly impressionistic rendering that seemed to magnify the stormy dabs of paint in atomic space; it did not reproduce the landscape photographically. It takes imagination to see beyond what's right in front of you, she scolded. Yet she did not see the impoverishment of our emotional lives right in front of us.

It seems to me that the shock of giving birth to me in Germany audited their sense that either of them had any real control over their lives, and between my mother's anger and my father's refusal to express anger about that night, when the German matrons did not let them build the proper foundation to my life, something ran afoul of expectation; that is to say, nothing happened. They went on as before. My father didn't roar at the hospital door like the tiger I know is in him or call the authorities after he was dismissed, unwelcome, and my mother, on her back or on all fours, like Satan raving but getting his bearings in the muck after God throws him out of heaven, well, she fought as she might, she gave birth to me that night, and after all the celebrations—her parents arriving from America, my sister staring at me with brown-bright round eyes, my father rolling along the tracks of his pharmacological career, making drugs that fix or mitigate what's not right in the body or mind, and the congratulations and mazel tovs arriving on schedule—it must have been true, no doubt it was true, it was documented all right, and the birth certificate proved they had created something good together.

My mother suffered. My father put up with her lapses because there was enough joy and belief in institutional family-unit happiness to be had. They believed in the pleasures of signing their names to a contract that proved they had found their center in their marriage, and they believed in irresistible children and an irresistible life. How many of us can look at that paper without the sour realization that we have documented our lives by pulping the lives of hemlock, fir, and pine? Like trees, we are axed, cudgeled, and squeezed into becoming; we are wood pulp transfigured, only a component of a society. The tree that was a coniferous, dendritic seed of knowledge is no more than a filing system for what would be better served by memory. Fool yourself, but your papers are proof of nothing.

My life grew so fast in that hospital room. It was invigorating and sweet to breathe the earth-air, to feel my lungs turning on like a nineteenth-century machine. Wind in, wind out. "The air tastes good to my palate," says Whitman. The atmosphere smelled like hair spray and starched cotton. My mother showed me a photograph taken at her wedding, so I would recognize my father when I met him. The imagery had drama because they were young, and because color, and the way film was processed, was different then. They were a unit, a pas de deux, the way you can't help being that unit when you are center stage, glissading across the pupils of everyone watching. In love, in that moment, you create, from the craft of your bodies, a person. Here was the love machinery of a mixed-race union of East and West. They had no idea what they were getting into.

I kept returning to the photograph, because it documented not their wedding but their love, in the angles of the room. This showed me how three-dimensional their love once was. The broad, flat white surfaces pulse with so many unknown colors and light wanting to be discovered but bound by the room's geometry. It told me how they had felt for an hour or two. And then what? After the guests went home and they were two? Their love-wedding was so unlike my own elopement, which took place one spring afternoon by a creek in a forested section of Central Park in New York. It was a long time before I realized that marriage was nothing but a document that led to a marriage contract and then a divorce contract, and in between the beginning and end was my baby, who was screaming.

Docēre, I think. What did they learn? What did I learn? How three-dimensional their love was. I will never know more than a handful of stories about them. I decide, in this moment, that if there were diaries or a video of me in that hospital room—being handed from one parent to another or picked up from my pram, any moment between May and July 1966—I'd be a different woman. This is merely my blindness to the magnitude of experience. What can I encompass?

"Encompass worlds, but never try to encompass me"—I wonder if Whitman was sly, because you cannot encompass worlds, and he knew it. Behind his tender bullhorn, he seems so lonely. There must be a point at which we embody love and boil ourselves in it, unable to love properly. I keep trying to prove with the documents that my parents loved me, just as Whitman keeps trying to prove with his lists that he—and vicariously, we—could abandon ourselves to a love so inclusive that everyone in society would be lifted up, but his sentimental encyclopedia of advice, jobs, injustices, and sexual desire makes me first enthralled and then bereft. *Leaves of Grass* is the grandest one-night stand in poetry.

The FS-240, or Consular Report of Birth Abroad, that my parents filled out on my behalf, three months after my birth, is a way of avoiding the truth: I have no status inside or outside any clear borders unless I consider my mother's uterus my original country. Because my mother was American, the United States handed me citizenship that was both guaranteed and conditional, which is an accurate summing-up of how, in my fifties, I see the world. The children of American citizens born abroad are granted citizenship, as long as their parents fill out the FS-240 and file it with the American consulate and as long as they live in the United States for five consecutive years at some time before the age of eighteen, when they legally become adults. We moved to America when I was seven. If my parents hadn't moved with me to America by the time I was twelve, in which country would I have become a citizen? Would I have been sent to the German courts or to the Indian courts, to claim citizenship in either country? Who would have fought for or against my becoming a citizen of that country? Would America disown me? Who would I be then?

I'm a fill-in-the-blanks sort of person, so I believe that each of the boxes on the FS-240 embodies all the possibilities of circumstance, pleasure, and menace that as an infant I did not know until they happened to me. Perhaps this is my first clue that I have no control over being, and limited control over the rhythm of my days in this world. There is not only Frankfurt, where I lived for five months, but other borders and cities in me. I can keep filling in the blanks with constructed narratives, to explain the accidents that others call fate; I do not believe in it any more than I believe in astrology or magnetism or the Year of the Tiger. I do believe in habit and imagination, and out of that you can burn your way into any narrative you choose.

I think that I am an FS-240 named Diane Mehta, a living document based on temporary status in a European country as the daughter of two foreign nationals, in a postindustrial epoch of new automation and thinking machines that know we have passed our threshold of climate, and high-speed internet or not, the land is hot, coastlines are picking up their skirts and moving inland, and even there, droughts, fires, storms, and heat waves are taking a toll.

How does that recalibrate the lives of you and me? I wonder if it is too big, in the way asteroids or volcanic eruptions are too big to ponder. When time wipes out a person, it makes you determined to find more, research forever, and come up with a proper plan for living. Looking back on the five mass extinctions, how do you feel about your petty concerns and your proof of citizenship here on Earth?

When I look closely at the FS-240, I notice that the Date of Report is July 18, 1966, at 10:30 a.m.—two months after I was born. The few dozen boxes on it tell me that people are expected to square their biographies in compartments, without expressing the seesaw of rage, pleasure, and despair that compose our emotional landscape, but we also know that it is our job to invisible-ink the boxes with epigrams that describe the skewering or lyrical memories that shade the address, occasion, date of birth, place of birth, and definition of national or foreign identity that persuade us that we are special or homeless or that the air we breathe—our shared atmosphere—is foreign.

This document that records the just-born children of U.S. travelers suffers from a failure of imagination. The address—listed under my mother's name, "same as husband," as if my father's document sufficed—was Westendstrasse 29, Frankfurt/Main, Germany. Harry W. Williams, vice consul of the United States of America, signed the document. I searched for the vice consul online, but there was nothing to track down. His life was missing. Frustrated, I did a search for my parents in the *New York Times*, and this brought the distracted satisfaction I craved, as if I could build out what I wanted to know about the important dates so the empty spaces didn't feel so empty, and because I know the tragedy behind whatever documents I could find, which is that they are so meaningful precisely because they are meaningless in that they are not the thing I want; I want to know what really happened in those first moments and days I was alive, and I want to know what it was like living with my parents in those months between the two documents that insufficiently describe the beginning of my time on Earth.

What promise I felt when I went into my prehistory and found the *New York Times* document announcing their marriage: "Dr. Dilip Jayantilal Mehta Weds Miss Carole Leonard." Did the writer realize that inasmuch as a man weds a woman, she weds him in return? Was marriage just a job? Did he pause when he read my father's name and think about how odd it felt to see, staring out from his handwriting at him, a knot of Indian and Jewish names? How miffed she'd have been to be called a "miss"—wouldn't she have been? Wasn't she not only a feminist but also a Mrs. Dilip Mehta? Hadn't she relinquished her name to be in the hitched-up unit the government requests of couples, and that couples expect of themselves? They had parents to please, and they looked forward, I am certain, to the small wedding they had at Essex House in Manhattan. She lived at 239 East Seventy-Seventh Street, and he at 1360 York Avenue. Justice Henry Clay Greenberg, of the New York Supreme Court, married them.

All of it seems promising, yet I sense, in my bassinet, that my parents will not be happy. I wonder what they felt about the epoch they occupied then: 1966 was a year of socially progressive and geopolitical realignment, over which the U.S. government attempted to exert control. Between my birthdate, May 12, and the date that the consulate issued my FS-240, July 18, Betty Friedan founded the National Organization for Women, which one year later endorsed the legalization of abortion and gave women the chance to achieve equal opportunities with men. The Indian nuclear physicist and Nobel Prize winner Homi J. Bhabha, who supervised India's development of nuclear weapons, died when an Air India flight from Bombay (now Mumbai) to New York crashed near Mont Blanc. (Or when the CIA, unwilling to accept India's nuclear program, assassinated him.) We moved into an apartment building near Bhabha's bungalow on Malabar Hill later that year. America was embroiled in the Vietnam War, and in those two months, time stretched out on a different scale because the death and bombings in two months of a failed twenty-year war are too startling to list. The civil rights era was under way in America, in the forever war between North and South. In *Miranda v. Arizona*, the U.S. Supreme Court guaranteed criminal suspects the right to be informed of their constitutional right to be silent before or after the police laid into them. Finally, Lasix, a drug used to treat fluid retention, or edema, was cleared for use by the FDA.

This is the event that is most personal to me. Lasix is part of my family history, a curative that my father talks about with excitement. He recalls the first use of Lasix (then known by its generic name, furosemide) by Indian troops, to cure the high-altitude pulmonary edema they suffered during the Sino-Indian War in November 1962. Troops were flown from sea level to five thousand meters in the Himalayas to fight a border dispute with China, and the Indian Army became hypoxic. Hundreds died. Chinese troops, already on the Tibetan Plateau, were acclimated. My father explains, in an email, that it was General Dr. Inder Singh who published a paper, in the *New England Journal of Medicine*, about how Lasix sped the recovery of Indian troops. India suffered massive losses in the month-long war. That doesn't tell you or me anything about the troops, or about the foolish trust of postcolonial India relying on its wits to build independent power. The government realized that Pakistan was not the only enemy and scrambled to build a more strategic army to become the power India would turn itself into. But those airlifts from sea level to altitude in 1962 left hundreds of stories buried in the Himalayan ice, drifting in high winds, evaporated and immaterial but alive in the fog. How did those trained soldiers feel when their legs swelled up and they found themselves immobile, stalled by their own bodies? What did they think of their training then?

I was unable to find any documentation except for a now-declassified document detailing the first world symposium on the effects of hypoxia in high-terrestrial altitudes, which convened in 1969. Sujoy Roy, professor of cardiology at the All India Institute of Medical Sciences in New Delhi, explained that he and his colleagues had spent five years studying acute mountain sickness among troops airlifted to eighteen thousand feet, into Himalayan terrain. It was not only in 1962 that pulmonary edema struck. India airlifted its troops into the mountains again and again. Just as Indians were dispensable to the British, Indians were dispensable to Indians.

Why does Lasix matter so much to me? The FDA approval of Lasix is one link in the drama of my mother's life and our family history. My mother took Lasix when her ankles puffed up with water, a side effect of heart failure when she was in her sixties. Lasix arrived on the market in 1966, the year I was born, and that small fact melts into the narrative, then still evolving, of how my father built his career developing drugs and bringing them to market—Diflucan, Zithromax, Viagra, Lipitor, Zoloft, Norvasc—and is a character in the years-long medical saga of how each of us struggle with illness and mark our bloody path with mitigating drugs. The narrative of my father's career delineates one way my mother treated her illness, and the approach of my father and the myriad psychopharmacologists who often turned to him for his expert advice while fiddling with the drug cocktails they served her. The last cocktail, concocted six months before she died, changed her utterly; she became less hysterical, and she lived out those months as an ordinary human who was dying. She died of heart failure because her heart was too big to survive. This reality—her heart—is the document in this story. Her ability to buoy herself with love, and spend it, shrank in proportion to the failures of her outlier heart.

Sometimes your body boxes you into a shorter story than you would write for yourself. If depression had not felled her, perhaps she'd have found a way to enlarge her love to the size of her giant, clunky heart, and I would not be bent on discovering her first sparkly moments with me.

My parents left Frankfurt five months after I was born, in October 1966, and deposited me in the arms of my father's sister in Santa Cruz, a Bombay suburb, for a month. They took my sister with them and stayed at the Ritz Hotel in South Bombay while they secured a flat to live in. My father was still working for Hoechst. He wanted to move into a sea-facing apartment in a building that Hoechst owned, in Colaba, the southernmost district in South Bombay.

In India, you bless a house before you move into it, in a brief ceremony called kumbh, and my parents performed this ritual for the Colaba flat, eager to move in. In a kumbh ceremony, the youngest virgin daughter carries a coconut on a tin adorned with flowers refreshed in a bowl of water, and walks around the house to offer a blessing. (This role was usually mine.) The ritual is a hedge against the disappointment you will inevitably feel in every house. Even now, my father's irritation boils over when he talks about this flat in Colaba in an email explaining that the company's medical director got the apartment instead of him. This was the home he preferred, and to which he had committed in the traditional way he knew.

The taxes on the Colaba apartment, owned by Hoechst, were lower than the taxes my father paid on the fifth-floor penthouse of the Gold Cornet building, which my parents rented on Gamadia Road, high up on Cumballa Hill and about ten kilometers north of Colaba. This is the flat that my parents discovered for themselves. It was in a far lovelier location, and it spanned the entire rooftop, which was connected to the interior through a bamboo deck, where they hung a swing, and this is where I had birthday parties and giant white cakes baked in the shape of the number that represented my age. We were a five-minute walk from the Arabian Sea—a short walk up a hill, on a peninsula between the sea and the bay—and from Breach Candy swimming pool, a members-only club and now-famous artifact of the British Empire.

Like many Indians with means, we grew up at the swimming pool, built in 1928 and shaped like India. It admitted only whites until Independence, at which point they let in Indians married to whites. (It wasn't until 1967 that Indians were permitted to be ordinary members rather than in tow to someone who was white.) In the sixties, my father was one of a dozen Indian men, including the movie star Shashi Kapoor, at the club. Sometimes the admission card tells only half a story, because we loved it there, and my mother was never going to stop being foreign any more than my father was going to stop being Indian. The same was true, roles reversed, when we moved to America. I don't know who felt more foreign in the other person's country, though I suspect it was just as strange to be an American wife in a Jain family in India as it was to be Indian in a New Jersey and then in a Connecticut suburb as the head of clinical research for a large pharmaceutical company where those visiting thought the boss was the man sitting next to my father, rather than my father himself. How quiet they must have been when, after pitching their services or product to my father's deputy, with all the eye contact and cheerful solicitations that go with it, the deputy turned to my father and asked for his opinion.

For my father, it's easier to associate memories with numbers, so the memory of our Gold Cornet apartment that comes to him first, and which our conversation hinged on, was the exorbitant tax on it, even though Hoechst covered his costs and shipped a Mercedes from Germany. My parents hired artisans to build the furniture and my mother filled the house with art.

My parents blessed this house, and in the end, my father says, he preferred it. From the roof, I could see in any direction.

I have known only one home in India, and I cannot imagine any other address, or how my life and my access to my relatives in it might have changed if we had not lived there. I would not have spent years racing the two girls on the bottom floor, children of the landlord, down the driveway, and given Monisha a head start because we were not evenly matched. I would not have feared and one day gotten captured by the strange, barely clad crazy man who lived on a board above the stairway in the garages out back, which housed not cars but a number of families. They were two stories high and decorated with colorful textiles.

If I hadn't lived in the Gold Cornet building on Gamadia Road, I would not have seen that horrible man's body under a sheet when he died, and the expression on the faces of the men in the garage when I demanded to see his body after they said he went to heaven and pointed up. I wanted to make sure he was dead, because he had often chased me. I would not have been on a pretty hillside where the roads wind up and up to Kamala Nehru Park, with its thrilling views east across the bay and west to the Arabian Sea, and near the Hanging Gardens, with its mythical topiary creatures organized around a central fountain, and street vendors selling bhel puri or ice cream, or training monkeys. I would be a completely different person if I had not lived on a hill two blocks up from the salt-dark sea. This was the address I loved. This was the place with ramshackle blue roadside temples and puddles of water where people bathed, and every day, I ran down to the corner to buy a paper cone filled with salty nuts for ten paisas, and I swam in the blue water in the pool the British built, because back then I knew who I was. It is only now, because I do not know who I was to my parents, and who they were, separate or together, that I am in search of my home, because my old home on Gamadia Road doesn't matter. But I can look around the corner at the absences full of stories. The documents are not even a quarter-share of truth.

My parents, Dilip Mehta and Carole Leonard, on their wedding day, May 11, 1963, in New York City.

Invisible Woman

The Mehta family in 1973 Bombay, on the day before we moved to the United States. Photo by Praful Patel.

When I feel most invisible, I turn to YouTube and watch videos of free diving. I became enthralled when I was researching the motions and rhythms of being proficiently underwater for a scene in my novel about my parents. I'd been watching videos of Esther Williams's synchronized swimming in 1940s aqua musicals and came across other swimming pool videos, which led me down a rabbit hole of clips of locals diving in Bali and Puerto Rico, floating effortlessly over corals and anemones without equipment, breaking the surface like dolphins and piking downward to explore the sea again.

I saw a Bajau fisherman slip into the water with a single breath and a spear gun and descend twenty meters to hunt on the seabed, emerging minutes later. One video led to another, and soon I came across people who weren't just reef diving without equipment but free diving as sport. There seems to be a kind of religious experience in all of it, whether you are spear fishing on the sea floor in giant steps, negatively buoyant, or descending into blue-black nothingness in a face-down drift. World-class free divers have highly specific in-the-moment feelings about it. Immortal peace, according to one. He said it forced him to live entirely in the moment.

When I started surfing YouTube in search of swimming videos, I was trying to imbue my protagonist (a version of my mother) with an emotional buoyancy, so I made her a gifted swimmer. In those blue moments, she'd be briefly fulfilled. The muscular romance of her body stitching the surface of the water would entice readers to look beyond her ragged edges and into the beautiful hurricane of her personality. But I didn't realize how depleted I felt, swimming for years in this story of an American fair-skinned woman who closely resembled my mother and who had so little to ground her emotionally. She didn't belong in India. I'd spent my whole life, since immigrating from India, feeling invisible in a shiny new country that seemed not to care much about me. Half a lifetime later, I still feel invisible so relentlessly that I think I have no choice but to embrace this invisibility as the real me.

I chose to give my character a proficiency that evoked admiration in public, and which made her, and by extension me, noticeable and worth loving. She—we—would be in love with who we were, from the inside of our heads to the outside of our bodies. So here I was, watching divers chasing a record—or something less definitive.

It was enthralling to slip out of my armchair and dive into an abyss. When you are thirty meters down, no longer buoyant, you put your arms down and drift. Signals in the body tell the blood where to go and the heart valves how to act. The body engages its reflexive longing to be amphibian; it recognizes the ambient underwater sounds that to our ears are always the same season; you hear the harmonics of submersive exhalations. Down in the amniotic dark, where antique water pulses, you can hold your breath for a record-breaking eleven and a half minutes or for nine ordinary months. You are a champion of extreme depths. It is where life is most isolated and profound.

A century ago, scientists thought that if you descended one hundred feet into the ocean, the pressure would kill you. They believed in the logic of Boyle's law, an equation formulated in 1660 that hypothesized how gases behave. Water is denser than air, Boyle's law states, so as pressure increases as you descend, your lungs would shrink and this would kill you.

We all have utilitarian gospels, sometimes grounded in science, that we transpose as religious, but the scientific method is only a systematic way of testing hypotheses until the same results repeat enough that you believe them to be true. Am I invisible? Ideas in science are uncertain until they are proven to be true, and they stay true until they are disproven.

As you descend, your heart slows to conserve oxygen and your spleen contracts. But, it turns out, the body adapts: when you reach the zone where your lungs shrink (because they are no longer filled with air) your blood vessels reflexively rush to your lungs so they do not collapse, and swell to fill the cavity. Without air, your body loses its buoyancy and you sink. Carbon dioxide and nitrogen increase in your bloodstream, and slowly you slip into a semi-dream state—all while in freefall. There are certain emotional truths about resilience that unscientifically have proven to me that pressure does not destroy you but instead gives you clarity.

My feeling of being whole began fading when I left India at age seven. The country is a color wheel of brown, and I faded in properly. The day before we left, our extended family gathered in the gray concrete courtyard of my grandparents' apartment in Sion, a suburb about ten kilometers north of our Cumballa Hill home in Bombay, and took black-and-white photographs. No one smiled in the photographs except my mother, who was American. It was not because we were all unhappy but because we were Indian. Sitting for photos was a serious thing. You were documenting a moment of importance, establishing yourself as a person of status, making a record to contribute to your lifetime-timeline of family events.

We create rituals for everything we do, which is another way of documenting the passing of time. Everyone had a turn in the steamy courtyard, waiting at length to be called and then organized in relation to whom they belonged. First, our grandparents, Ba and Bapuji, with their six children. Then the entire family: the youngest children sat in the front row, older cousins stood behind us, and behind in the last row were our parents, with Ba and Bapuji at the center. All the brothers and the one sister look almost identical, with pronounced, sleek cheekbones and hair oiled into fine curves around their brows. I always thought that my father was the most beautiful of all his siblings: cheeks bright as apples, eyes quick to see what others didn't. After a time, my parents, my sister, and I were called. This went on all day, in various combinations. It was proof that as a child, at least in India, I was not invisible.

I possessed picture-perfect status as an individual in a traditional family: a female descendant of Gujarati merchants, a rabbi born in Minsk, a couple from Poland, and an umbrella salesman and a seamstress from Tarnov, Austria. I was one in a dozen cousins and a niece of many; I was a student at the well-to-do Cathedral—an Anglican private school where I learned embroidery and Hindi. I lived in a country at latitude 19 degrees north and longitude 72 degrees east on the surface of Earth. I was a girl with opportunities because my father worked for a German company so his wages were generous. I was a passive participant of rituals in a minority religion that largely exists outside the Hindu-Muslim religious conflicts that have bloodied the history of Indian culture and that, seventy-eight years after Partition, continue to fuel mob lynchings.

To whom does the idea of India belong? To which country do I belong? I do not belong to Germany, where I was born and lived, as an infant, for five months. India shaped my sense of myself and gave me a childhood full of other children. It gave me Amar Chitra comic books, which vividly illustrated the violent and provocative tales of the epic *Mahabharata*, and invited me to partake in the colorful frenzy of powder-throwing during Holi, the parade of Ganesh effigies heading to the sea on men's shoulders during Ganesh Chaturthi, my family's solemn Jain rituals and chanting, and monsoon rains that flung down cascades and battered hot pavements.

Something faded, figuratively, from those photographs later. Perhaps my sense of myself as Indian diffused without the smells of salt air, diesel, betel nut, cotton, and roasted cumin, and without the Ferris wheel of family and social events—but the girl I was then disappeared into the shag-carpet, two-story home with a dungeon-like basement full of ghosts and murderers on Woodcrest Drive in New Providence, New Jersey. During high school, I worked at a drugstore that stocked outdated, dusty boxes of condoms and Lancôme makeup that I sold to girls who were prettier than me. I was a disaffected teenager and obsessively ate the chocolate bars on the shelves across from the cash register to satisfy my directionless cravings and my inner rage that I did not have a CoverGirl face and I did not look like everyone else in the small Catholic town we had moved to.

Next door to the drugstore, the supermarket had wonderful polygonal metal cages, with an invisible top, on wheels. My sister and I filled it up with Frosted Flakes and Fruit Roll-Ups. We wandered like queens among packaged food, fresh peaches, and melons. I was invisible in the sprawling aisles of the supermarket unless I stood in line at the deli counter and pretended to transfigure into a number waiting to be noticed, and for my numerical identity to be yelled out and given human form.

My parents gave me a new identity in the canary yellow cage that was my room, with its sateen floral bedspread and gold-detailed white princess desk and cabinet set and a goldfish that swam circles in its own cage. My mother told me I was Jewish and instructed me that from then on I would attend Sunday school at Temple Sinai in Summit, one town over. Perplexed and irritated that I had to give up a weekend morning, I complied and I got myself a minimalist Jewish education, ignoring the teachings about history and God and enjoying the social interactions with boys who, unlike my peers at school, didn't shun me for being Jewish and Indian—and who showed me how to get high. I loved the Purim carnival, especially the cacophony that transformed the gym when someone yelled out the name of villainous Haman. But more importantly, there were concession prizes for everything. No one ever walked away a loser at Temple Sinai.

During long high holiday services, I counted red hats to stave away the boredom, even when Rabbi Biel (whose sermons my mother loved) was talking. We were part of the community because we were Jewish, but we were not part of the community of our street. It bothers me now that the synagogue welcomed us not out of love but because our mother was Jewish. But back then, I was grateful to be welcomed in. To most people, I had the wrong color skin and the wrong religion. They thought I was ugly and I believed them.

Kids at school called me names: jungle bunny, spear chucker, kike, nigger. I shrugged off the minor insults from jerks and jokesters who said "ooga booga" or—with their hands cartoonishly tapping their mouths—made vulgar imitations of ululating Native American war cries in my face. I saw some relevance, even excitement, in the idea of being a tribal runner. I was proud of being a sprinter, faster than the fastest and most popular boy, Barry Blackwell, who I'd shamelessly beat in the final heat of a race for the annual Presidential Fitness Awards, a national competition. I was fleet, a characteristic in those first two insults that suited me. I was grouped in with everyone that Westerners called "savage," but apparently I had some extra-human tactical skill they lacked. My legs were long and brown; I was Mowgli in the forest.

But Rudyard Kipling's wolves were more welcoming than the wolves at school. Girls drew together in a mob to tell me off and pissed on my clothes during gym. Boys muttered as I passed. "Kike" was used less often because I could hide being Jewish, but when it arrived, the word was a knife. In *Western Wind: An Introduction to Poetry*, the poetry critic John Frederick Nims describes the "k" sound as a stop, plosive, or explosive, along with fellow "p," "b," "t," "d," and "g" consonants. These are the drastic consonants, he says. "They cut off the air for a moment, let pressure build up behind the barrier of lips or tongue, then release it with a tiny explosion."

In the galaxy of the English language, violent expletives persist.

But you can voice half the dialogue, even if the other part is rubbish and hate. The rest you escape in your imagination.

The first time someone called me a nigger, I had no idea what it meant. I was riding my Schwinn bicycle with a pink-flowered banana seat and butterfly handles from which streamed shiny pink tassels when I flew into the wind at full speed. I paused, one day, when a boy down the street yelled out from his front patio, and planted my feet on the ground in front of his lawn. When I saw a rock leave his fist and head my way, I moved my bike over to dodge it, but I stepped right into its path. "Nigger," he yelled. I went home crying, my head and hair all bloody. When I told my mother what had happened, I asked her what the word meant. She asked if he had called me that and I nodded yes.

What does it mean?

It is a bad word for Black people.

Am I Black?

No.

Am I closer to white or closer to Black?

White.

There was an edge in her voice. My mother was a fair-skinned Ashkenazi Jew who married an Indian man. I still wonder why she answered that way. I don't know if it was racism or if she was worried that I'd be forever harassed for the color of my skin. Maybe it was wishful thinking that outside this small town, I could pass, and so, for me, color would not be a disability. That incident taught me that no one can be trusted to tell you who you are (not even your mother), and that everyone has their own version of your humanity.

When I was a child in Bombay, I took swimming lessons at Breach Candy Swim Club's indoor pool. Lessons got me nowhere and this had an impact on my ability not only to swim but to follow rules later. I dreaded getting in at the deep end, and climbing down the stairs cascading down the inside of the pool, because they dropped off midair and abandoned me. I worried that as I sank, the water would capture and steal me. I was only just beginning to have a proper conversation with my body and didn't want it to disappear.

I preferred the outdoor pool shaped like India, where Bombay's expat society and Anglo-Indians gathered to crawl over the sun-sparkling blue surface, beguiled by easy geometries of sky, water, and, just a few meters to the west, the fifty-million-year-old Arabian Sea. Admission to the swimming club was closed to Indians, unless you were an Indian like my father, married to a white woman like my mother. A refined, chocolate-skin local man, he was wildly visible to the whites at the pool but would have been an invisible member of the club—that is, not a member at all—but for my American mother's passport. Outside the pool, it was she who was perpetually visible, with milk-white skin beneath knee-length wrap skirts and bare-shouldered tops. All this in a city where he was invisible in a sea of similarly chocolate-skin Indian men married to sari-clad women.

We also belonged to the Officer's Club, at the tip of the peninsula in South Bombay and twenty kilometers south of our home. (Breach Candy was down the street.) It didn't have a swimming pool by the sea, but they admitted Indians, and what it had on Breach Candy was acreage and trees—I loved riding my marine-blue three-speed bicycle along the water—and the chance to "swim" in the sea. Bobbing in the choppy water was dangerous and exciting, and it made me feel as if the whole world was shaking me inside its bottle of energy. Like all children at the club, I'd descend the slimy concrete stairs covered with seaweed, inside a life buoy tied to a rope hooked to the dock, and slide in. How quickly the sea, even at its calmest, turned fortissimo around me. I doubt I ever stayed in for longer than five minutes, but those five minutes were filled with emergency and possibility, and they have lasted me fifty years.

An Indian man treaded water beside me in case the rope broke or I slipped out of the lifebuoy. He had no lifebuoy. I always wondered how he had developed the Odyssean swimming skills necessary to battle the currents. For years, I had recurring nightmares in which I fell into the ocean and disappeared. At the edge of every peninsula and every seam between land and sea, the sea violently pulls at land from underneath, a reminder that we are fishermen, mermaids, and wrecked sailors who depend on the bounty and mythology of the sea.

When I watch these free divers and swimmers on YouTube, in the blue light of my computer screen, I wonder what it is about being underwater that does not frighten but intrigues me. That breath-holding balance in the bardo between the surface and the galaxy below my feet is where my flesh and bone become liquid. Vast conversations pulse by in the compassionate water. The sun falls with me, the sky rises above me. There is the temperature of the water and the temperature of skin and the absence between one and the other is the motion of my brain telling me that it is connected to my arms and synapses are firing inside my eyelids. I can talk through centuries to trilobites and octopuses inching by with tales of marine history. I am immersed in a body of water that resembles the soft cavern of a body, and there I am radically calm. My purpose is fixed.

I believe that we are always looking for ocean because we feel safer in anything that resembles a womb—before life gets to us and before we lose our facilities to take it in. Approximately four billion years ago, some biochemists believe, human life began in a fit of enzymes and four-hundred-degree heat from a hydrothermal vent in the ocean. We emerged, amphibian, from the oceanic abyss. This was the original womb we transmogrified in.

When we are just a cell in the womb, we have a genetic footprint already, but physically we start at zero. This is the process of becoming. The engine of our mothers' bodies fabricates our eyes, feet, fingerprints, heart, and lungs, and assembles the building blocks of our personalities. What is hardwired and what is influenced is not yet determined.

When we moved here in the seventies, there was only one Asian grocery nearby—in Springfield, New Jersey. It had only been a decade since Asians were allowed to immigrate to the States. In 1965, the government passed the Immigration and Nationality Act, which removed the 1921 national-origin quotas keeping Asians, Arab, African, and Southern and Eastern European immigrants out.

The Asian grocery in Springfield was run by a Chinese couple, but all the Indians flocked there for bunches of fragrant coriander. You couldn't get it in supermarkets or greenmarkets because the former had never heard of such a thing and the latter didn't exist back then. There was Hostess and Entenmann's and the Fruit Roll-Ups that the vegetarians relied on, along with potato chips and Doritos. If you asked for coriander, surely you were speaking in tongues. But in the Asian grocery, you were wrapped in the language of immigrants, which is food and transactions, but undergirded by the possibility that your little store would last as long as you could thrive in this country of giant homes and square green lawns that needed fathers to man the lawn mowers under summer sun and shape the tiny lawns that fulfilled the expectations of the neighbors. You lived the tidy gift-wrapped life of people who understand that the boundary of a driveway is a line you do not cross unless you intend to call attention to yourself. By staying within the confines of your cage, you make yourself an invisible Asian so the rest of the country does not have to let your smells and clothing in.

Every few weeks, we returned to the Asian grocery in our Chevy station wagon to sift through the dusty products that had journeyed oceans with stories like buried treasure: canned Alfonso mangoes recited tales of the poet Mirza Ghalib eating eleven Alfonso mangoes, one after the other, shirt off, before turning to drink and couplets. Basmati rice from Dehradun recalled the sharp turn where a city bus flew off a cliff and how a young boy replaced his dead father at work, cutting stones from the slopes so the government could build new roads. Bags of dal evoked the smell of aunties who fed us soft nutritious moong, with ghee and jaggery, when we were sick.

Other East Asian children roamed the South Asian aisles, and seemed to find the same exotic appeal in Ayurvedic tonics and curatives, bright-yellow ghee, and colorful bags of aromatic spices that I found in their packages of noodles and magical jars with calligraphic logograms refusing to translate themselves and offering, instead, rough illustrations of peppers, beans, plums, and tamarind.

We were there not because we cared about one another but

because we craved the same items for our kitchens, the center of our homes. In the grocery store, Asians shared muted greetings over bins of ginger that connected the topographies and climates of Asia. There is no ginger like that of an Asian grocer. It is plump and knobby like your knees when you grow older. The ginger is twisted like DNA but similar to a ripe cantaloupe in scent and fullness. The desiccated imitations of ginger that Americans learned to appreciate showed up in supermarkets decades later, so overlooked that the ginger was almost invisible.

After the visit to the tiny, one-room Asian grocery store, with its conflictingly exciting fragrances and hustle-bustle people, we switched back into being not-Asian in-betweeners, in our suburban lives where we subsisted on mix-and-match dinners of boiled green beans in a bag, Beans and Franks or Salisbury steak, and except for special occasions when we had tandoori chicken, we assimilated into the seasons.

If you grow up in a sea town between seasons of tropical light and walloping monsoons, like me, it is bewildering to switch to the American Northeast, where punctual snow conjures hieroglyphs and blizzards bear down their cold, hard Puritan facts. Seasons are doubly extraordinary: the freeze releases, lakes crack and pop, and the air grow warmer until it boils with summer, and lifts when the procession of backpacks and chatter spark the streets. This excites the trees into the colorful expressions of children, before they, overwhelmed with what they have learned all year, shake their orange, yellow, and red castanets—goodbye, goodbye.

Every home is imperfect, and implicit in all art is the wrenching longing for home and the love of your parents taking tender care of you in that home. For a long time, I was on a seesaw: nostalgia for India and my sun-saturated childhood running with my cousins in the rain or eating chapatis as they flew off the stove. I remembered these days after we moved and I began to battle my self-esteem in a land that did not befriend me, in a town that seemed so spacious and empty.

In India, you are seldom alone, and as a child, I never wanted to be. Bombay is a jam-packed singing honking screaming banging city with pockets of calm, and when monsoon comes it washes away the world and races through the streets like bulls and plows people down with it. Rain scissors into everything around you and blurs eyes into mustaches and saris into streets. The blindness of water is rejuvenating—and we are all invisible. Suddenly it lifts and again you can see. An hour later: cascades drumbeating again. Those were the best times to be outside, when the rain became sparklers around our bare feet.

I loved the city's frenzy of activity and other children. So much of my life was lived on the street, in impromptu sprints down our driveway with my landlord's daughter Monisha, who was slower than me, or feeling the sun full-tilt on my face on Chowpatty beach eating kulfi or riding camels or hand-cranked Ferris wheels at Juhu Beach, or even just chasing my cousins in an empty lot, because home is about the life you live with other people, not the house itself. In India, our home was the fifth floor of an apartment house, on a road that runs up from Warden Road, which abuts the Arabian Sea just north of Breach Candy Swim Trust, and ends where it runs into the north-south thoroughfare of Peddar Road. With our parents, we'd drive south along Peddar Road to Hanging Gardens, a topiary garden at the top of Malabar Hill, adjacent to my nursery school and its attendant church. If we were with the nanny, we'd walk the mile and a half south along smaller streets, which took thirty minutes. At the Hanging Gardens, people of all sizes, colors, and stature strolled in the evenings and watched the sun spill into the sea.

In America, you are always alone. On my first drive, as I stared out the windows of small-town northern New Jersey, I found myself wondering where all the people were. The giant American home or aspirational mansion was an abyss of loneliness: large rooms, one for every purpose, and quiet streets that protected you, like King Kong fences, from apocalypse. There was so much space that was hyperorganized in acre-lawns on lots blueprinted onto the municipal map of home after home after home. I memorized who lived where by the curve of the road, the colors of the house and shutters, and the inviting flowers that the wives planted out front. But not everyone wanted our family to come in.

Wonder came crashing into my life in unpredictable moments outdoors: caroling with a friend at Christmas, sledding down backyard hills after snowstorms, playing flashlight tag in the cul-de-sac by the woods where a train on a ridge almost killed me while I was collecting pretty stones on the tracks, and where I witnessed, on two occasions, men masturbating. But it was worth going into the woods to run beside the creek splashing along to its aqueduct. Muddy embankments softened under my feet. Dead Man's Tree, leaning forty-five degrees in a clearing, invited children like me to climb up and bounce on it as if we were riding a camel.

Whenever you begin a new life in a new house, you must first bless it in a small ritual called putting a kumbh. The process of the ritual entails circling the house, which brings peace to all corners of the house. It is a Hindu ritual that my Jain family adopted—Jains often adopt Hindu rituals because they have so few of their own. My first experience of kumbh was on an astrologically auspicious date and time in the fall of 1977. We had been in the United States for five years when my father sponsored his sister's family. They moved to Maplewood, New Jersey, a twenty-minute drive away. It was a middle-income town with narrow backyard plots and the wonky Union Mall, where retailers hawked goods in a maze of stalls: silver-plated necklaces with my name in script and posters of Farrah Fawcett (to me the embodiment of sex appeal), whose feathery hairstyle and breezy smile were unsuccessful models for my own.

I was asked to perform this ritual because I was the youngest girl in the family. Girls are considered good omens because they are innocent. My aunt had placed, on a round, stainless steel tray, a hairy brown coconut. It, too, is a good omen. The contraption was similar to a Carmen Miranda Tutti-Frutti hat, but without the glamorous pineapple and without her party attitude.

We started in the backyard. Neighbors leaned over the fence, grinning and pointing. I was a vision to ridicule: a girl balancing a pot with a coconut on my head and repeating prayers in Gujarati with a trail of dark-skinned people following me. My blood boiled at the offense of being a sideshow, but never for a second would I have avoided the ceremony.

The coconut is a reminder that whatever happens in life, you must remain hard outside and tender inside. You should be cool-headed instead of angry. You should be soft and nice, and avoid bad feelings for others. If you go to a temple in India, for example, you will see people buying a coconut from a vendor near the entrance and giving it to the priest or laying it by the entrance as an offering.

I have a photograph of my father, on a trip we took to India together, walking confidently toward a small, colorful temple with a coconut in his hand. He wore a navy-and-white-striped short-sleeved American shirt with a blue collar, and blue pants with a belt. There was something touching about the way the coconut swung from his hand as he walked. That temple compelled him to leave my side and perform a ritual he had grown up performing. His spontaneous but deliberate act possessed an air of childlike excitement; he was repeating a ritual that had for so long become a memory.

I performed the kumbh for each of my father's siblings, after he sponsored them, but there were no such blessings for our home in America. There was my mother's Judaism and its communal Sabbath pews. Just as my mother gave up her life in America to live in Germany for six months and India for seven years, my father gave up his rituals to pursue, with quiet courage, a better life as an immigrant in a country that would rip him from everything he knew.

The aunt whose house I blessed reminds me now that because we believe the ceremonies will bring us happiness, we forget the principle behind it. She is probably right; we decorate and ritualize our homes in ways that make us feel good, but we forget about the idea of home itself. Every house or flat she lived in was sparsely decorated: firm beige furniture, a table for the central event (the meal), a refrigerator stocked with fingers of ginger and large batches of coriander chutney, firm beds, and plywood desks for my cousins to achieve straight A's in.

The interior life is something you cannot ritualize without a little deception and a little hope. Perhaps we all think we have done our best. We put the blessings in the right place and provide proper instruction. In between, we pray in a kind of ritualized hope that we will succeed, and when we do not, we try to mitigate our losses with other things. I think the principle that my aunt was talking about was to do your best to set up a home and keep a hard shell between you and the outside world, especially when you are an immigrant. You can make a decent home and try to feel lucky instead of cursed. You can buy the freshest coriander available at the Asian grocery before it gets too crowded on Saturdays, and you make a thousand coriander chutneys for the thousands of chapatis you will eat. How lucky are the children who find peace at home. Tenderness, a room where you can place your keepsakes and sort out your confusing life, a place where you feel safe, a womb.

My aunt has said that rituals like kumbh will not help you. She is a woman who goes against the tide of ordinary religious output and feeling, and who forms her own opinions.

So I wonder: When my courage is at the edge of what I can withstand, what if I explore the trouble? My lungs can expand to hold pockets of air to help me breathe, and it doesn't matter if I'm invisible, because it doesn't matter what other people see.

Greeting Cards

At age ten, I became a salesperson of some importance. I traveled door to door in my suburban neighborhood and sold greeting cards from a blue trifold brochure illustrated with airbrushed winter landscapes, Victorian homes, red-cheeked children, and cats.

The trifold brochure presented all the activities I would ever love, the houses I'd occupy, and the people I would meet. Selling cards gave me access to a community of plump, middle-aged suburban women with short brown hair who invited me into their homes, even when their children did not, and who gave me the sense that while their husbands were sitting in offices, in their ironed white shirts and striped ties, they were doing the important work of choosing greeting cards to celebrate occasions that would arrest whatever disasters were happening. They were the kind of women who believed that a young girl ringing their doorbell with a sales pitch was worth listening to, but I also knew that I was offering them something unusual because of the consistency of their reactions over many seasons, and the fact that they studied the illustrations with love, and like me, they were enamored. I suspected that it was rare to drop everything for a half hour in the middle of doing chores. It made me feel that life was worth it because more often than not, the doors that seemed closed to me would suddenly open.

What we knew, which their husbands and children didn't, was that greeting cards were the embodiment of love on paper, and you could sell that love or buy it. The transaction made us part of something greater than the timid streets we lived on and our limited opportunities. Money exchanged, and my one-dollar commission, put us in charge of the marketplace of feelings that galloped across state lines in a white envelope with weight and firmness.

A greeting card proved that whatever else was happening in your life, someone cared about you. Inside the card with the beautiful illustration, your correspondent had scribbled genuine thoughts and signed their name. There was an expenditure tied to it, in the form of a $0.14 stamp, along with the expenditure of time walking to the post office to mail the card.

The greeting card was history itself. The colors of the artwork and the mood it created stitched communities together during ordinary times and times of desperation. All of my clients looked forward to the day when I showed up with a new catalog. Unlike the men who occasionally answered the door and said no thanks without asking what I was peddling, the women were invested in time passing. They anticipated occasions. They knew that the card created emotional suspense from the moment a card was mailed, like a secret, to the day the card was opened with surprise, and read and received with appreciation. This was a secret society that relied on the postal service and the phone. Your friend would surely pick up the phone and call to thank you for the greeting, and that was the beginning of a longer conversation.

Chanting with Ba

It took me a long time to realize that when my grandmother chanted, she was having a conversation. A vague mystery hung in the perpetual heat while my extended family stood there, facing a photograph of the emaciated Jain prodigy and scholar Shrimad Rajchandra, and listened to our grandmother's voice. Her scratchy alto had a rugged undertone, with the hint of a chuckle in the higher register. Ba, as she was called, delivered the verses in a methodical manner. Her phrasing paralleled the familiar sounds of other kinds of ritualized chanting: a muezzin's call, a cantor singing, choral music, church bells, sirens, mothers yelling out the window to their children and calling them home.

Ba's face was round as a tin of gingerbread cookies, and she never wore makeup. She parted her hair in the middle, smoothed it back tight, and twisted it efficiently into a bun. I loved watching her dress, half-outfitted in a tumble of soft white cotton petticoats and tops as she sat on her bed, combing her long mane of oiled black locks, smelling of powder and starch. Her handsome face is replicated in the polished movie-star facial structures of her children.

Jainism defined Ba's presence in the slow, sturdy way she walked, her devotion to the rigors of prayer and chanting, and the self-imposed restrictions on her life, such as days of fasting in which she took nothing but boiled water. The purpose of the fast is to control your mind instead of letting your mind control you, explains my aunt, who has tried to live a life equally devout, even if as a statistician she is more scientific than her mother. The logic works like this: fasting lets you get rid of some old karma and collect good karma, and it trains the soul for salvation because the soul is after everlasting salvation. Food is one of many worldly pleasures. "The quality of the soul is to know things," my aunt says. So the ritual is a kind of training for the soul in search of infinite knowledge—achieved by renunciation. Chanting helps you get through it. It's an admirable way to think about things, though my Jewish-Jain idea of the soul is not their idea of the soul. My imagined soul is one that's full of feeling, not free of feeling.

Jains don't believe in God—neither the Judeo-Christian kind nor the ancient Hindu pantheon—but they revere these saints for achieving nirvana, at which point they are godlike. What Jainism shares with Hinduism (the majority religion in India) is the idea that if you collect good karma, you are reborn into a better being and eventually can achieve nirvana. In Hinduism this social climbing is inextricably tied to the caste system: an insect is reborn as a dog, a low caste person moves into a higher caste, a woman in her next life becomes a man. But because Jainism has no caste system, it is through acts of karma and renunciation alone that a person attains nirvana, breaks the bondage of the life cycle, and becomes a saint. In Jain cosmology, twenty-four men have reached this stage.[1] They are known as Tirthankaras, the most recent being Mahavira, a contemporary of the Buddha (ca. 500 BCE).

My grandmother didn't have much interest in religion until her oldest son, Chandrakant ("moon"), died in 1959. She never got over Chandrakant's death. After he died, Ba turned increasingly devout and began reading about religion, morality, and ethics. According to my father, his grandmother had always been devout and had led prayer groups in Bombay. As a child, he and his siblings listened to several prayer songs daily, but there was no tradition of chanting back then. Ba and his grandmother used a mala, similar to a rosary

1 Jains believe there were many more Jain saints before Mahavira. (Not all saints are Tirthankaras. Some may be on their way to becoming a Tirthankara but are not there yet.) People assume Jains don't believe in God. This is true if you assume that God is the creator of the world. Jains don't believe in a creator. They believe that although there is no creator, the "pure soul" is God—or godlike. For convenience, modern Jainism dates the start of the religion to Mahavira's lifetime and teachings in the sixth century BCE.

My grandparents and their six children in 1952 in Rajkot, a city in the state of Gujarat in North India. My father is on the right. Photographer: family friend named Kishor.

but with 108 beads, during the prayers. My father, like many Jain children, learned the Navkar Mantra, the most basic Jain chant that children learn when they are young. It comprises nine two-word prayers paying respect to others who have reached higher stages of spirituality than you.

When I asked my father about the Navkar Mantra, I was shocked to find that, even in his early nineties, he mutters it to himself before bed, not out of religiosity but out of habit. He'd done it for years, along with counting numbers and square numbers and other "difficult and repetitive and boring things," as a way of getting to sleep.

The habits that punctuate our daily existence add structure and stability to our lives in part because habits are ostensibly devoid of emotion. Your arm reaches out in the way it is accustomed and wedges a spatula under two eggs, which it balances briefly before the precarious flip. Salt is dispersed. A fork is retrieved from the drawer that will slide in and out however long you live for, and unthinkingly you eat. We rely on the rituals that make us feel safe. But beneath each thing is something extraordinary: an egg is a semipermeable membrane composed of calcium carbonate crystals and a forty-protein albumen miracle surrounded by opaque chalazae ropes clinging to the glorious orange-yellow yolk, all warmly hatched from a two-legged feathered hen. How deliriously inside-out moments can be, if we realize what bubbles underneath them.

If you care about something, you make time for it. Besides her children, Ba's prayers were her life's work. Maybe chanting gave Ba some remove from the travails or social interactions that so define modern life, or perhaps it genuinely offered calm, like meditation with music. She was so deeply entrenched in living a Jain life. But if it all started as a gesture of grief for Chandrakant, did she believe that somewhere in her prayers, and in her voice, her son was still alive? Was chanting a foil against feeling, or did it liberate feeling—in the way that a classical sonnet structures yet liberates feeling in the macramé of its tightly woven rhymes? We have infinite bonds with our children and our childhood.

My father's recitation of the Navkar Mantra in recent years calmed his mind, and maybe it made him a little sleepy. He led a secular life and had a secular Jewish American wife. (After she died, he married a British woman who practices Zen.) He recited these mantras as a child and again as an old man. How could this practice not evoke memories of a past life? He lights up at the chance to talk about his childhood, so maybe, for those five minutes of chanting, he slips into the comfort of being a child again, praying with his mother at night. I believe there is some childhood in him. I used to sing the Hebrew round *Im tirtzu ein zo agada* ("If you will it, it is not a dream") to my son at bedtime, and he sang the Hebrew words with me. I learned the song at synagogue, when we moved from Bombay to New Jersey, and I have held it dear since. Although my son is twenty-one now, maybe when he is old, he will mutter it to himself before going to sleep, and he will remember me.

Secular Jainism was such an accommodating religion in my family that I still don't understand my relationship to it. If I want to practice, I am Jain. If I do not practice, I am not Jain. My most devoted relatives work Jain prayer into their lives the way Americans build churchgoing, yoga, or fly fishing into their lives—though this in some mainstream way seems to be true for most moderate Hindus, Parsis, and Muslims in India, too. Religion is not a costume, and it does not define you. For Jains who yearn to be devout, it is a strict path to achieving *moksha* (freedom from rebirth: nirvana), but for others, it accommodates your willingness to engage or not. You can be Jain, like my father, in spirit if not in practice. There is no on or off button, no conversion ceremony, no study requirement. It is human-led, a matter of devotion, like needlework or parenting or an apprenticeship for brick masonry.

The variety of Jainism I was taught involves trying to be a good person and to avoid doing harm.[2] You do what you can. Our biases and desires lead us to different versions of what harm is. But chanting somehow seems to remove all these concerns as you do it. Time feels suspended, words hang on the air, and the pace of life slows to the rhythm of prayer. I think of time as a rowboat in our universe, and chanting is the sound that oars make. But I do not see why the oars are not, say, a spider's web, a sound wave, or pi, the geometry of the world.

My aunt points out that chanting is easy. It can be done on the fly, and you don't need to be physically or even mentally fit to do it. You don't need money. Five minutes is fine. Chanting is not an end in itself. This kind of devotion is harder for me to understand than the secular devotions of the body, like sex or love, or the devotions of the mind, like reading or writing or the bloom of imagination, and dreams of stairways and tunnels. Chanting forces a pause in the routine, and the recitation of words occupies your mind as they absorb the time. Is that what training the mind is? I know what

---

2 My takeaway from growing up in a Jain family was that being a Jain hinges on nonviolence. The concept is not only material. It does mean one must avoid harming all forms of life, from people to insects to root vegetables. But at its core is the even more meaningful goal of avoiding doing harm to other people through your actions or thoughts. Mahatma Gandhi famously adapted Jainism's tenet of nonviolence and used it as an organizing principle for a decades-long civil disobedience movement to purge the British Raj from India.

training the mind to love is—it is about learning to feel. I have always assumed that chanting was the opposite, the practice of putting feelings aside and an enviable compartmentalizing.

One of the main tenets of Jainism is ahimsa, or nonviolence—to avoid destroying life or harming others. But I am suspicious that the renunciations of Jainism are effective as a way of staving off the violence of feeling. For my grandmother and her children, Jainism offered a way to keep emotions in check. You can fast to exhaustion, chant to focus the mind and calm the breath, and repeat the phrases that meditate you into believing that everything will be fine. None of this will preempt emotion; you try, my aunt says, not to be angry, but you may still be angry. There is also a detachment from care that you pay for in your relationships with others, as if you can unbutton your problems like a shirt that can be put in the laundry.

Chanting is a gesture of my childhood, and it is a comfort, despite the fact that I do not do it. There is a deep, pained yearning embedded in it that has something to do with Ba and her starched cotton petticoat smell and my mother's Jewish songs that I learned at her New Jersey synagogue and Poconos summer camp, sitting in the amphitheater that slants down to a glassy forest-rimmed lake and a striking, voluptuous woman with chestnut Rapunzel hair strumming acoustic guitar on a wooden stage. Chanting has something painful to do with Lamaze and the breath, during the ravaging if ordinary labor of my son's delivery. It is similarly in tune with the rhythm of song that evokes that hard-won feeling you dissolve into after, say, twenty hours of laboring over a poem or forty hours of fiction and then the moment briefly hits you, and you're in that breathless groove of confident exactitude and suddenly there are garlic and sapphires in the mud and four seasons in you.

When I lived by the sea in San Francisco, I commuted to T. S. Eliot's singsong recitation of his masterpiece, *Four Quartets*, which got stuck in my barebones Toyota Tercel's cassette player for three months. Eliot's meditation on time, written over six years, is loosely structured around the four classical elements (air, earth, water, fire) that reflect the four seasons. When the junky cassette player broke and started playing, on repeat, a poem about time, it started as a funny refrain but then became annoying. Aggrieved, I considered my options: suffer in silence or listen to Eliot over and over. I chose Eliot.

Those thirty minutes I commuted each way evolved into a time I lovingly anticipated as I raced along San Francisco's Great Highway. I passed Ocean Beach, populated by surfers and fishermen, and merged with Skyline Boulevard by Fort Funston, where hang gliders hovered above the cliffs, and finally I eased onto Route 1 along the coast, through fast-moving curtains of fog at thirty-five miles per hour—the safest speed to continue forward while the reliable winds swept the fog aside. As I drove south of San Francisco, the fog receded or swirled back out to sea and the skies opened up as I cut east and upshifted onto sunshiny Interstate 280, the road of all people, not my half-secret coastal detour.

Through fog and big blue skies, Eliot still chanted for me. "Garlic and sapphires in the mud," we'd intone together, dropping our voices an octave at the mimetic mud, and I'd smile at the piquant regularity of this phrase that dug into some guttural place in me, physically and verbally, before releasing me from its depths and into the long pause that lifted into soprano moments. For sixty minutes a day, I listened to the *Four Quartets*' incantatory rhythm.

> Words move, music moves
> Only in time; but that which is only living
> Can only die. Words, after speech, reach
> Into the silence. Only by the form, the pattern,
> Can words or music reach
> The stillness, as a Chinese jar still
> Moves perpetually in its stillness.

That passage from "Burnt Norton" says that time is fluid, but you can move through it in ways that are meaningful if not permanent. During those months of driving, Eliot's chanting became my chanting. Perhaps my recitation was empty of spiritual meaning, but his playful, plaintive rhythms had spirit, and we were having a conversation.

The American Eliot himself was disillusioned, his life marked by nervous breakdowns and domestic anxiety. His conversion to

Anglicanism while taking British citizenship grounded him—though the philosophy of the *Quartets* is a mixed bag spiritually, with a wide-eyed nod to the *Bhagavad Gita* ("Song of God") in India's Sanskrit Hindu epic, the *Mahabharata*. The *Gita* is a dialogue between Prince Arjuna and Krishna, avatar of Lord Vishnu, creator of the universe, on the battlefield. Arjuna hesitates at the prospect of killing his relatives in this war between two branches of his family, but Krishna, disguised as his charioteer, persuades him to fight out of duty. It's the fruit of Arjuna's action that's at stake: the soul requires action to attain enlightenment. Mahatma Gandhi, the architect of the nonviolent resistance movement that won India her freedom in 1947, said the *Gita* was a metaphor for the inner struggle. But how do you tend the soul?

The *Quartets* offer no resolution but are a literal path through a rose garden and a spiritual path much like the one Ba was on and which my aunt is also on. They are a pursuit of a higher experience—but what is the nature of that experience? Neurologist Robert A. Burton, who studied consciousness, says there are neural correlates for emotional responses, but it's not clear what sensations and responses define experience: "I know the brain creates a sense of self, but that tells me little about the nature of the sensation of 'I-ness.' If the self is a brain-generated construct, I'm still left wondering who or what is experiencing the illusion of being me." Reluctantly, he says, it dawned on him that the pursuit of the nature of consciousness "is driven by the same urges that made us dream up gods and demons, souls and afterlife."[3]

It is difficult to imagine we will ever know what consciousness is, given that the only tools we have to decipher it are our own brains, and that feels like a chicken-and-egg situation. Burton has tapped into better questions: Why must we know? "Theories of consciousness are how we wish to see ourselves in the world, and how we wish the world might be," Burton says, the implication being that we will

3 Robert A. Burton, "When Neurology Becomes Theology: A Neurologist's Perspective on Research into Consciousness," *Nautilus Magazine* 49 (June 15, 2017).

never know. What does that say about why I've been chasing the story of my parents, and of me?

And it makes me wonder, when it comes to Ba, or my aunt, or any religious Jain seeking higher experience, what do we transcend, and where to? I do not understand Ba's spiritual feelings, but I do understand the way she cooked for us and laughed; put her dentures in a cup of liquid that fizzled, which fascinated us; and brushed her inky black and white hair. Ba's devotion seems hard on the intellect in the way of all religions: you question your faith, you demand answers. But I wonder if the ability to achieve effortlessness in prayer is any different from other rituals of faith.

There is no philosophy that will imbue you with the feeling you seek. You must dig up that feeling yourself. I am more than a little enamored of Eliot's idea that words, after speech, reach into the silence. Going to temple isn't going to buy you enlightenment, but will prayer and chanting help get you there?

Thirty years ago, I asked Ba if she'd change anything in her life, and she said that she wished she'd gone to more parties and bought more jewelry. She grinned and her dentures sparkled. I didn't know how to respond. Her reply was ironic, I realize now. She had no interest in those things. But she respected the life choices of others and she understood the desire for fun. One night while visiting Bombay in my twenties, I had a standoff with an aunt because I wanted to go to a party with some Indian guys from London who I'd met on the plane. We argued insufferably. Ba cut in. The room grew quiet. "Ba says, 'Go, have fun,'" translated my cousin. I grinned at Ba and went to my party, where I had a miserable time trying to look pretty.

My aunt says she also has not achieved the effortlessness described in Rajchandra's prayer *sahajätma swarup paramguru* ("The individual whose soul is in its own original form without any effort is the best teacher.") even with more than half a lifetime of study, various renunciations, and plenty of chanting. For years, she has returned to India to study with three Jain female monks in the town of Khambhat in Gujarat. She met them, with Ba, when they delivered a sermon in 1987. She stays with them during her visit, to see how they live and to learn from them. Because they are Jain monks, they have no possessions and are entirely supported by the community, which invites them into their homes for meals and pays for their medical needs.[4] Their job is to preach to society. The most senior woman gives a *pravachan*, a sermon on scripture, in the morning and afternoon. In the evenings, the teaching is informal; they give my aunt notes or books to read and they discuss them, talking for hours. She has gone to remarkable lengths to advance in her journey, motivated by her gurus, and to become a more nuanced practitioner of Jainism.

But that feeling of effortlessness has eluded her. The concept eludes me. Does it feel like concentration, or the way flying feels for creatures with wings? If it is akin to muscle memory, I suspect that it is weighted heavily to memory, because the brain is stronger than the body. We all want life to be effortless.

My only reference for understanding this sense of contentment or effortlessness is a physical one: desire. In India, arranged marriages sometimes blossom unexpectedly into love—in many cases, from habit. It's a kind of proof: we love what we are familiar with more than we despise it—love is effortless when it is cumulative. Human events punctuate time passing, which convinces me that Burton is right: it is our tireless quest for answers about the nature of consciousness that motivates us.

The atheist philosopher Daniel Dennett says that consciousness is an illusion, a cheap trick. The brain has its mechanics to which we attach the idea of consciousness. We write our Everygod books and endow those humans with superpower status. We set up rules for followers, who fund our churches, temples, synagogues, mosques, and retreats. That doesn't mean there's no higher purpose or that we cannot transcend ourselves, only that we mark what is religious in human ways—because we are schooled in the ways of people who say that God speaks through them, but we are not schooled in the ways of God itself.

---

4 A small number of Jains are ascetic (monks); they are supported by the Jain community, and some preach or are itinerant. Lay Jains practice with varying degrees of commitment.

I believe this, but I also believe that Ba and my aunt are onto something I will never understand. I prefer to be attentive to experience, instead of figuring out what experience isn't. When I'm in India, a Muslim call to prayer creates a tiny rush of adrenaline and then a calm in me. It is a marker of people putting aside their worries, chores, work, and turning away from themselves. In a Jain temple, or when listening to relatives pray, I drift. I watch the person's lips, follow the vowels as they move across the stone floor, and feel time passing. Sounds become beautiful, like Ba's alto voice.

I look out the window repeatedly while at my desk and observe that trees are moving. I watch them for a while, and remember Virginia Woolf describing wild-moving clouds in her brief, brilliant book *On Illness*. If she had not been ill, she would not have noticed the clouds. We have not slowed down enough. My dad's habit of reciting the Navkar Mantra has lasted his entire life, so I wonder if his atheism is itself an act of devotion.

I do not need to believe in God to practice the work of the soul. When I was younger, I'd listen to a song hundreds of times to ride its rhythm in the poem I was writing. The lyrics and music took my choices away and let my mind latch onto sounds, and then I organized those sounds in language. Within the poem, anything could happen. It was similar to those months with Eliot stuck in my cassette player, and similar to chanting. I became immersed in a moment, guided by words, and free of attachments. Suddenly it made sense: because it is repetitive, chanting leaves no space for the mind to wander.

No, said my aunt. In the first stage of chanting you are still involved in worldly things. In the second stage, you push those away. In the third, you begin to ask questions: "Why am I saying Ram, Ram, instead of Diane, Diane? You think of what Ram did." Most people end here, in the middle. "It is the beginning of the next stage that you think about your guru. What is good for my soul? Is there a soul?" The serious work of the soul is when chanting becomes intellectual. It's like the first time you read a poem and you have one set of feelings. Later you get a more elaborate meaning.

For example, my aunt avoids eating root vegetables because if you pull up the root of a plant, you destroy its life. My aunt learned from those Jain sadhus that there were thirty-five vegetables to avoid, and not only roots. She had not heard of twenty-seven of them. But the question about what is good for your soul is a fluid one. A potato will die if you pull it out of the soil, my aunt explains, but you can replant it or put it in water, and it will grow another tuber. On the other hand, argues my cousin, her daughter, you are taking the source of its life to feed yourself, even if it grows another tuber.

When Ba chanted, in her apartment in Sion (a suburb of Bombay), we stood around her while her voice ambled a cappella over the syllables with which we'd grown familiar. She faced a photograph of Rajchandra, devout and emaciated, cross-legged in a loincloth. He lived inside her white cupboard and came alive with incense and our gaze. I wonder if she was reciting this prayer, from his letters:

> He prabhu he prabhu shu kahu, dina nath dayal
> Hu to dosh anant nu bhajan chu karulal
> Oh Lord, what can I tell you, you are very kind to everyone and I am full of mistakes.

My father says that as children they heard that prayer nightly. For me, one prayer is as good as another because I'm not looking for meaning. But when Ba chanted in Gujarati, time felt suspended. Am I also full of mistakes? Chanting is free. You only need five minutes. Why don't I do it? Why only with Eliot?

I have no attachment to Jainism, and no attachment to Ba's prayers. But mumbling along to them, decades ago, gave me a chance to feel Jainism in what is arguably its truest form: practiced by those in the middle of prayer.

There's something about music and repetition that makes me feel privy to some sort of collective experience. If the nature of that experience is hotly contested by philosophers, it doesn't matter to me. My soul is troubled. I am full of mistakes. My soul will never be free of desire, because desire is the only place where suffering does not exist for me. I suspect I have misunderstood the teaching entirely.

Her Greatest Hits

My mother was no spendthrift, but her mind was rich. She loved going to the symphony but wouldn't splurge on season tickets to the New York Philharmonic or the Metropolitan Opera, even on my father's seventy-thousand-dollar research salary, a knockout for an immigrant in the seventies. She shared the cost of opera seats with two friends. Like her, they were teachers and children of the Depression. She was always a little starved. She hungered after Beethoven, Mozart, Haydn, Wagner, and Bach. Her fervor revolved not around her children or husband, or even around being Jewish. Her love hinged on listening. But what did she find, and what was she looking for in the first place?

My mother died when I was thirty-five. During my childhood our pleasures harmonized around going to the symphony. This promised the magic of tunneling east below the Hudson River and emerging in twilight in a city that had extruded itself from bedrock into a collection of silos and reed pipes. We left at dusk, between sundown and first stars tearing their way into retreating light, and raced to spotlights and historic sounds pressed into the wood paneling of Avery Fisher Hall at Lincoln Center in Manhattan, the home of the New York Philharmonic. We were going somewhere important while daylight was still in motion, and by the time I returned to our night-sky driveway I would have violins and trumpets in my bones.

The philharmonic filled me with the sense of possibility and the romance of a glittery life where women performed in slinky evening gowns and heels and rich girls wore velour dresses with red sashes and tied their hair up with plaid ribbons. The minutes of practice and adjustments before the conductor walked out felt like an intimate part of the show, chaotic and lavish. My mother, an educator by training who had stopped teaching far too early, would quiz us before the overture started. I'd work hard for my mother's praise, which I'd secure by identifying instruments, by sight or sound, in the orchestra. Violins were easy but a cello or bass demanded more of my attention and an educated guess. Trumpets were smaller and deeper and rounder in sound than their trombone cousins. How proud I felt when she pointed at a sound in the air, and I slid into the voice of the saxophone that paused there. Chords and melodies blew through its shiny brass body. The harp gave us pause—it was a giant antiquated instrument, cousin to the thousand-year-old lyre with roots in Ethiopia, Iraq, Scotland, and Wales, yet here it was. A bassoon seemed to come from the Serengeti itself.

When my mother tired of this, she explained what conducting was. For the same work, conductors took different attitudes. This was astonishing news. Each conductor had their own conversation with the music. This was the beginning of my awareness that I could become a fuller person by understanding how different artists approached the same piece of music. This perspective would later benefit me as an artist. Entranced by the magisterial auditorium, I felt struck, listening with strangers. A live performance sent shivers across my skin. This secret language of chords, counterpoint, C major, D minor, fortissimo, tension-heightening half-step sharps, and semitones. My mother was rapt, and I was often too frightened to look at her because the moments there seemed so intimate. My father slept. Rhythm raced like adrenaline through my mother's operatic blood. Electrified, her eyes and ears seemed blue-fire red with possibility. In these extraterrestrially tuneful moments, I felt the unbearable desire of love, if only for collective sound and not for people. After the finale, my mother leaped up, clapping: *Brava!* She screamed with all her might and that crooked half-smile relayed omniscience, *Brava! Brava!* She never stopped clapping.

The return home was always the same. Fragments of what I had just heard played in my head while we entered and emerged from the Holland Tunnel onto Route 78 in New Jersey and raced west in silence. My father navigated our green Chevy Nova along smaller and smaller streets. Neon flickering traffic lights and octagonal stop signs screamed at me in terror. We pulled into the driveway where the pop and crunch of rubber tires on gray arrowheads of suburban-industrial gravel announced our arrival to our white .034-acre wooden house built in 1965, which had been waiting patiently for us all evening. A square home for round-peg people. Its saving grace was the maple tree out back, whose roots knotted a dugout filled with large rocks to leap along. I'd collect the leaves, which had five webbed fingers and brushed velvet skin, and examine the holes left by sap-sucking caterpillars and other critters. Omens of beautiful ideas to come, these marvelously outsize leaves turned blood-orange when they were nearly dead. Life crumbles in the yard before it blossoms again.

My mother ignored the moon reflected in the car window and melting at our feet. She ignored its display of magic on the grass, at rest after being decapitated all summer when my father mowed the lawn. Winter curled around my ankles and crawled up my skirt as I stepped out of the car. "First one in pajamas wins!" She flung open the front door and sprinted up the stairs in her black shimmer-shammer gown and double-wrap twenty-two-karat necklace of gold filigree balls jingling, sweet scent of Chanel in her wake.

I was determined to win. I'd march out proudly in my flannel Lanz of Salzburg nightgown, which felt like Christmas Eve, which I longed to celebrate. I smelled like laundry and buttons. There was my mother, victorious in her bedroom doorway.

She looked younger in her nightgown on those evenings—lit from within. It was as if she had briefly abandoned the clothing, lipstick, opinions, hair spray, costume jewelry, and thinking-silence she'd built around herself and suddenly was a proper mother who loved her children and functioned with ease in her middle-class life. Other nights, she was not so vivid.

Lanz of Salzburg nightgowns are made of the softest brushed flannel. Under the button-front placket with eyelet trim, and below the bodice, the material billows, wide as the frock that Laura Ingalls Wilder, with her rebellious freckles and strawberry braids, wore on *Little House on the Prairie*. My nightgown had green medallions made of tiny leaves and red and blue hearts and flowers. The pattern repeated itself up and down the gown, positioned between the stripes along which "Lanz of Salzburg" scrolled sideways down the body. It tattooed decorations all over me. I turned into a gift.

We bought the nightgowns at a small independent department store one town over. This is where I bought the Brownie and Girl Scout costumes that made me feel as if I were going to military camp; a training bra, which came in a box; slacks in wide-wale green corduroy; and a garnet-and-navy check blouse with a scalloped collar that made me feel handsome even in braces. On one outing, I found a Lanz gown that was part of a more contemporary line, with bold, saturated colors in place of the lake blues and half-serious pinks. Here was the thrill that life promised beyond the small-town Catholic values that seemed so constricting, the town that did not welcome me, and the classmates who called me names.

When I held it against my brown skin, it didn't matter that like many Indian girls I had shadowy fuzz darkening my philtrum above my upper lip. It didn't matter that I had knotted, frizzy curls. It didn't matter that I was not beautiful because I was only a vehicle for the nightgown to be exhibited. The blood-bright gown called attention to itself and invested my teenage body with possibility. Red was an insanity color, all tongues of fire and throbbing Old Testament rage. Red showed up in every season: apple, tart cranberry, botanical rose, and the glossy candy cane of women's lips when they left the house and demanded to be noticed. A red nightgown presented the possibility that I, too, might be worth admiring.

I wasn't a fit for this small New Jersey town. I wasn't a fit for anything. My mother encouraged me not to become a writer: a waste of time, a hobby, not a job. Be a window dresser or a marine biologist. Go into "the sciences." But the rules and functions of science and math were lost on me. In mix-and-match chemical formulas, I saw temporal objects, born in flasks over Bunsen burners, that had other intentions for their brief lifetimes beyond showing preteens how colors change. A flame dies out, smoke disappears. Fire, that remnant of antiquity and Prometheus, is proof that more knowledge is always behind the scenes. Teachers pretended to have all the answers, but a deeper logic was locked up inside the chalkboard. If you existed in the third dimension, an A student, you understood the rules. If you existed in the fourth dimension, like me, the rules were confusing—I was interested in experience, and I could not understand the facts. At the end of the semester, I took home a memory of the pretty chalkboard and a lot of unscientific confusion about beautiful equations and a report card with a C.

My mother slipped on her nightgown after dinnertime. Her breasts swung a little in the bodice and I wondered if that was the style of all adult women, and if I would ever fully be a woman. It seemed curvy and strange to have extra sections of you that a nightgown didn't bother to organize with zippers or clasps or structured waists. It was the opposite of math, which on its computational surface feels buttoned up. Your body could move like a lava lamp inside the nightgown and gain or lose ten pounds and the nightgown would cascade from your shoulders just the same. The flannel was so thick that it would keep you warm even if you ventured out to watch icicle daggers thicken on the eaves of your home after a snowstorm blew in and the temperature plunged. It was in my red Lanz nightgown that I mattered to my mother most. When I wore that nightgown, which made me feel beautiful, I felt certain that my mother finally thought I was beautiful, too.

My mother was serious. She was a surly Brooklyn Jewish intellectual whose spontaneous and playful moments after the symphony were the chance of a lifetime. What did she like? Prune hamantaschen, white eyelet blouses, cottage cheese, Jim Lehrer, and drawing trees and naked women sitting on the corner of a bed. What did she want?

As evidenced by titles that she cataloged in a spiral-bound notebook and which listed the books she read over a ten-year period, one thing she seemed to want was sex outside her curdled marriage.

The list throbs with longing, and the works on music are really about pleasure itself.

Here is a handful of titles that my mother recorded reading, among dozens of others, in the fall and winter of 1980:

Wagner, Panofsky
Richard Wagner, Taylor
Richard Wagner, Gutman
Beethoven: A Pictorial Biography, Valentin
Celebration: The Metrop. Opera, Robinson
Elektra libretto, Strauss
Portrait of a Marriage, Vita Sackville-West and Harold Nicolson
The Adulterous Woman, Camus
The Courage to Live, Ari Kiev
The Ring librettos: Wagner
Speak, Memory, Nabokov
Tristan and Iseult, Bedier
Hamlet, Shakespeare
And the Bridge Is Love, Alma Mahler

That fall, she read Bernard Malamud's *Dubin's Lives*, his last book and the one I love most. A biographer struggling to start a book about D. H. Lawrence plunges into an extramarital affair, a nod to the idea that in order to understand Lawrence you must embed yourself in his life, and live it—but it's no accident that it is yours already. More proof: Vita Sackville-West and Virginia Woolf had a heady romance going while married to men, and Alma Mahler, off in a spa while her husband the composer was dying, fell in love with architect Walter Gropius, who sent Mahler a marriage proposal that got routed directly to her husband himself.

Desire has its consequences. My mother weighed those against her need for more affection, but she seems to have stifled this, and projected it into life-affirming music while thumbing through great books about the problems of humankind, along with others about adultery and its costs. In Camus's "The Adulterous Woman," Janine, the lead, finds her satisfaction not in the soldier she spies on a bus but by venturing into a fort in the middle of the night and laying on her back, enraptured at, by, the sky. We demand that our bodies give us the visceral pleasures we deserve, but the joy we seek is interior.

Around the time of my mother's reading list, a lot of romance was on the radio—as well as plenty of adultery. Blondie's "Call Me," the title track for *American Gigolo*, was number one. If there was a real number for a Richard Gere escort who loved satisfying middle-aged women, I'm certain my mother would have called it.

I was also looking for satisfaction. The winter of 1980 was a time of my own first crude, if viscerally felt, romances. It was the era of disco and I was fourteen years old. Michael Jackson had three hits that year, a short afro, glittery pants, and rodeo hips, and to me, he was the sexiest thing on the planet. In Billboard's year-end Top 100 list, the songs that stand out are "Shining Star" by the Manhattans, "Desire" by Andy Gibb, and "Working My Way Back to You" by The Spinners. All of these songs mourn love lost—or they demand more love. They were easy songs to rock to, and whether you were consumed or crushed by love, they were danceable and cheery. This provided a different picture of love than I saw in my family. You could pine away after a lover while the song uplifted you. It implied that love was always a hit, and in the wake of losing it, music was there to comfort you.

That winter of 1980, my mother also read critic Harold Schonberg's book *The Lives of the Great Composers*, a fact I discovered on the day I was reading Schonberg's successor at the *Times*, Anthony Tommasini. In his general-audience book *The Indispensable Composers: A Personal Guide*, Tommasini says that implicit in the general-interest books for music lovers Schonberg produced was "the assumption that music lovers cared deeply about 'greatness' and that we all knew who the truly great composers and performers were." Tommasini said that he took "the educational component of being a music critic seriously," and that his project came out of the realization that "many people who consider music central to their lives admit to knowing little about its inner workings." He saw a "hunger for insight," and so he set out on a Top Ten Composers project. "As I admitted from the start, the very idea of a top ten list was absurd." He asked readers to weigh in, and some music lovers dismissed the idea as "outrageous" or "dangerous and despicable," while other readers said "that, though engrossing, the series was frustrating, because they sensed I had much more to say about the composers I discussed." And he did—he decided to explore the issue of "greatness" in *Indispensable*. All of it gave him a chance to figure some things out. *Indispensable* was a chance to discuss "what makes some extraordinary composers indispensable to me." Tommasini seemed to enjoy nudging people into conversations, with one another and with him, about what they cared about most.

"What do you love most?" is a moving target of a question. Answers vary and new loves take precedence, but we try to sum up anyway. Schonberg for my mother learning about composers, Tommasini for me trying to figure out what I was hearing, Tommasini reflecting on Schonberg's mission, and everyone tackling big questions: What is great? What are the greatest hits of life? How do you gain influence? How do you become more loved and less dismissed? How do you become indispensable?

I started listening to Beethoven's piano sonatas, occasioned by a date with my partner at a recital by pianist Judy Huang at Carnegie Hall. Jerry had sent me a list of possible activities to choose from one Wednesday, as agreed on, in anticipation of spending time together that Saturday. We were planning an outing to create more meaningful moments together in our busy lives and torqued interactions. My choices: Cooking 101, art glass crafting, Ludwig Kirchner exhibition, John Singer Sargent Portraits in Charcoal exhibition, a trip to the KGB Espionage Museum, pianist Judy Huang in recital at Carnegie Hall, and the New York Philharmonic playing Salonen, Bach, and Hindemith at David Geffen Hall.

I chose Judy Huang because she was playing Beethoven. I never liked Beethoven. I'd dismissed his music as bombastic and thunderous—not nuanced enough. His symphonies refused to become background music and enraged me for being violently unpredictable, and they reminded me in personality of my mother. She loved Beethoven, and I never understood why. I existed in only half of her life, yet I have all of mine to fill in the blanks. The facts I have to work with are so limited, but maybe I recognized that in his way, Beethoven would help.

Huang would play the following: six Scarlatti sonatas, Beethoven's Piano Sonata No. 31 in A-flat Major Op. 110, Beethoven's 32 *Variations* in C Minor WoO 80, Tchaikovsky's Dumka in C Minor, and Liszt's Hungarian Rhapsody No. 10 in E Major. Huang, who had looked bored with Scarlatti, came alive when she began playing Beethoven's Piano Sonata No. 31—and so did I. There was a lot happening at once. It was not the Beethoven I had expected. If I was looking for something to shake me out of my growing dismay that I was not getting back from my life what I was putting into it, this was it. I could feel Jerry feeling what I was feeling, both of us sawed apart in our own solitary ways. I was glad he was there. In those twenty minutes, I slipped into some sort of apotheosizing fever that I am still trying to understand, but I know that people have moments of deep listening that changes what comes next. I felt pummeled, like strings inside a piano, by the small felt hammers Beethoven controlled when he pressed the keys on the other end of the lever.

This set me on a course of listening to the sonatas for the next few months: on the streets, at home, at work, in the elevator, on the subway. I longed to buy a piano, crawl inside the music, and figure it out. The chestnut-colored baby grand of my childhood waited for my body to slide onto the bench and open the page to C. P. E. Bach's Solfeggietto. It's a relatively easy piece for piano students because you only play one note at a time. The toccata, from the Italian *toccare*, "to touch," is all about fast-moving, light-fingered dexterity. For amateurs it is an achievement and for experts it is a warm-up. I was a serviceable pianist for five years, though in possession of no special talent. Even as an amateur pianist, it was enthralling to connect notes fluidly, to climb up and down the keys and execute an entire composition, and to feel pleasure at my muscle memory when each note entered on cue. I still miss being the person in whom a tune emerged.

One evening, I listened to a *Gramophone* podcast with pianist Jonathan Biss, who was discussing his experience recording all thirty-two of Beethoven's sonatas. When they took up Opus 111, Sonata

No. 32, the final sonata, the interviewer said quietly, you must realize there are people in the audience who are hearing that sonata for the first time.

Maybe it is only when you don't know what you are listening for that you find what you were waiting all along to discover. I put on my headphones to listen to Sonata No. 32 for the first time.

While I was married, I lost my access to music and my independent spirit, too. The CDs I had collected were shoved to the side for my husband's pop bands, and I lost track of where everything was. But even then, listening to music was painful and brought emotions flooding in that were entirely inconvenient for a life with a new baby. We all give up something to parent our children, but I gave up everything. My CDs slipped to the back of the pile, and in the process of shelving my needs to prioritize those of my husband, I just stopped listening. It took a divorce seven years into the marriage and seven more years for my son to become a teenager before I began opening my ears again. Sometimes it is difficult to figure out how to belong in your own family.

One night, we were walking around a park in Saratoga Springs, New York, and he offered me one of his headphones so we could listen to music together. Soft jazz flooded my ears. After that weekend, I promised myself that I would go to the symphony again, just like when I was younger. I would bring my son. He was at the age when he no longer wanted to hang out with me, but he agreed to see Brahms's *Requiem*, which I promoted as an hour long. I had given myself permission to listen to music again, and he enjoyed the performance.

There have been only a few before-and-after situations dramatic enough to change my life. Before my mother died, time was open-ended. After she died, the world came into high focus. Before my son was born, I cared for others in limited or temporary ways. After he was born, I felt elation again, and learned to love in new ways.

There has also been a before and after Beethoven. I'd been doubling down on my efforts to locate my tender feelings inside a romantic relationship. I had chosen Beethoven accidentally and not at all accidentally. I went because I thought I might not like it, and something about that made me impatient with myself, so I gave it a chance. No one ever told me how to feel better, how to appreciate music, or how to learn what love is. Beethoven was not a composer I discovered through my mother but in spite of my mother. Listening to Beethoven now, I am beginning to understand her joyful experience of his music, and understand why she preferred listening to music rather than listening to me.

While I cannot tell you much about Sonata No. 32 itself, I can tell you that four minutes into the second movement, he starts swinging, and it feels peculiar and confusing. He goes on for a time and the chords get fuller, jaunty, as if I were listening to Scott Joplin—but this is one hundred years before ragtime exists. Suddenly I'm dumbstruck, and lost, inside it, wondering what the hell he's doing. Beethoven had been deaf for years by then, but just like I returned from the symphony with violins and trumpets in my bones, when I was young, he had the piano in his bones when he was old. He put this sonata in the world using sounds he had memorized over years, and whose tones he understood—he was deaf, but he heard them in his mind.

We spend our whole lives learning that we already have everything we need to survive. We torture our spirits and try not to bleed out, hoping that we have gambled on the right life with the right people. We rack up failure and disappointment and disbelieve what we demand of ourselves. We are never good enough. Beethoven didn't do this. He worked tirelessly and revised his work, in his sketchbooks, to get themes right. Even the simplest notes crush expectation. Now I am a good six or seven minutes into the second movement of Sonata No. 32, and he levels those chords up, orchestral, colliding and renegotiating time, and some kind of harmony, before narrowing again into a lyric.

I hear what he is saying: wretched pain, jazz, tenderness, death, love, difficulty, romance, work, unrelenting passion, rebelliousness. What I hear, when Beethoven races along the edge of what seems possible in music, is the music that I played for so many years on my piano, serviceably but enjoyably. I hear the sound of my own weeping in shock at what he accomplished and at having missed the chance to listen to him all these years. I hear, at age fifty-three, for the first time, genius. I hear more things than I can follow and more than I imagine. I hear all the doubt in the world and none of the doubt in the world. But I doubt I will ever have another conversation that rivals this one.

Pianist Daniel Barenboim says, about harmony, that the difference between a conversation with words and a conversation in sound, with music, is that in music it can happen simultaneously, and one voice does not have to wait for the other to finish.

What we want Beethoven to tell us is that our lives are meaningful even when our relationships are not. That our conversations yield joy, discovery, kindness, closure, clarity, complexity. That our parents love us dearly. That the conversation is not one-sided—all the musicians are there, warming up before the overture. That there is more to discover beyond love. I don't believe it. It is not inaccurate to say that we are lost and uncomfortable much of the time. The rest of the world, or your children, may think your life is ugly, that you have not accomplished much, that you are ordinary, that you missed your opportunities, that what you've read, and how, misses the point. Too bad your greatest-hits moments of life according to the consensus didn't create nobility or compassion in you or make you famous. Too bad, too bad you didn't do enough. You're an emotional shambles. It is in your bones, it is unusual, and it does not come by often. Everyone is talking. It is 1822 and 2020.

What I hear in the chords of my mother's life, now that I have listened to Sonata No. 32 hundreds of times, is that in her forever-sadness was a life not fully lived. I have no proof that this is true, except what she showed us on the outside, which is only half the person.

I know my mother was not as whole as she would have liked, but her desire was not empty. Those sonatas must have filled some of it. She had undeniably intimate moments with music when love did not come crashing down the way it did in her marriage. I am listening to thirty-two sonatas in which love does not come crashing down. I have gone more than two decades without hearing her voice.

Part II

Making Love out of Memories

Year of the Dog

Dear REDACTED,

I'm writing to inform you that you have a terrible way with people. We hired you because you offered predictability in a hectic world. Each day you have sent a different person to walk our dog. We've been polite about it. Imagine if every day you came home to a different husband or every day there was a weird substitute for your onion bagel. But I like variety, you might say. Well, imagine that your substitute for the onion bagel was a kishka and you were a vegetarian, or that the different husband you came home to every night smelled like a kishka, and you were a vegetarian. Dogs like consistency and so do I. You're supposed to send a regular person on a regular walk on a regular schedule.

When I hired you, I told you about the migraines. Daily for seven months. I'm not sure how old you are, and whether you've had children, but a full-blown migraine is like childbirth in your head. Put in dog terms, imagine a ferocious, rabid dog inside you and clawing to get out while you are on all fours and crying.

A two-hour window for dog walking is just the edge of what I can handle. One of my migraine triggers is waiting. I have learned to avoid situations in which I am waiting, and now here I am, stuck waiting for Mr. or Mrs. Kishka of whatever aptitude or variety to arrive. It is not okay with me when people are late. Neither is it okay for my new dog.

This dog has gone through a lot. We got her three weeks ago from a shelter on Canal Street in Chinatown. There we were, looking at a dog that had been shipped from a Miami shelter during the hurricane, and the vet record says she was spayed over the summer. Because of her nipples you can see that she has already had pups. She is only two. I have my good guesses about her past. She has this odd habit of sitting in the dark, in our bathroom, and I wonder if confined spaces and odors are reminiscent of life in a puppy mill—and then, after losing access to her parents and her children, someone kicked her out of the house as if she were a pregnant teenager. Hired hands corralled her, and she got shipped in a truck with other lost or unwanted sorts and sent to New York City.

Last week, a new dog walker who looked like a serial killer showed up. I asked my son, then thirteen, to stick around just in case. The walker came in and I said a friendly "Hi!" but his eyes grazed the floor, finally making eye contact with a throw rug. He had another dog locked outside on a huge chain that doubles as an S&M contraption—don't ask me how I know this, I just do. He looked dirty, not like a kishka but like a burrito with a mop of knotted dark hair and droopy jeans. I had to put a password on my computer and hide the watches and my checkbooks before he returned. I shouldn't have to worry when I hire a service. I need normal people in my house. I have no idea if there are three, eight, or twenty people on rotation, and it stresses me out.

Will the next guy have a Weimar-era haircut or a Confederate flag tattooed on his forehead? Will he be a pornographer with a greasy smile that oozes lube and tacit vulgarities? Do I have to say hello? Then he will get the wrong idea. There are dirty people with poor hygiene and poor judgment and I do not want their sicknesses or their evil. You haven't mentioned if you do background checks on your walkers. I can't afford to wonder. I need a proper dog walker who will not arrive with an angry face or make my dog sad. People have so much anger and they will put their pain on me. Will they kick my dog? Will they set her free?

The migraines are oppressive, and I'm on the anti-epileptic drug Topamax, used off-label for migraines, for a few months. The hope is that it will buy me enough headache-free days per month that I can fit into the clinically proven category of migraine sufferers who respond to the beautiful little Botox shots in their head. These next few weeks are critical or it's back to the beginning. I've had only seven headache-free days since Jerry and I returned from Italy to blissfully cool weather. Because of the mentally ill dog and the unpredictable dog-walking situation, the migraines have been lingering—so on days when I don't have a full-blown migraine, I often have 20 percent of a migraine.

So, Italy. We (really it was me but, okay, *we*) planned it for five months, researching one country and then the next, trying to figure out just the right vacation. Ireland was too rainy and cold, Greece was hot and had too many homogenously picture-perfect sand-and-water islands, Croatia was inconvenient transit-wise, and Peru too up and down with the altitudes. I'd gone to India alone last summer so we hadn't been away together alone since Paris, right after we met. Italy was supposed to be grand. We went to Lake Como but it was when the heat wave hit and the migraines were at their worst. My third neurologist put me on prednisone three days before we left. It's supposed to kill migraines when they are unkillable. It started working, but the stress of the day-before-travel boosted the migraine and then the flight, exhaustion, and the first night I could've slept, my son called in a panic from fencing camp, where he was in a room alone and terrified because some prankster left a note in his desk that said: "Whoever sleeps here shall die tonight," and he didn't care that I was on Italy time. Then hours of phone calls for another few days with the guy who ran the fencing camp and was threatening to send him home, which would ensure the total destruction of my son's self-esteem and his fencing career—if he didn't stop panicking. After several ragged days—and I'm not good with jet lag anyway—I flipped out and threw the house keys at Jerry when he couldn't explain why the AC wasn't working. "It's on," he said. "No, it is not," I said. He kept talking in some philosophical way about air-conditioning that was Italian "on" versus American "on." "What do you mean Italian 'on'? It's not *on*," I said. "Precisely, but in fact, technically it is," he said. "Not like in America where it's continuous AC."

I screamed like a harpy that he should leave our house, though of course, we weren't in our house, we were in some villa right out of *Garden of the Finzi-Continis* on the northern end of Lake Como in a town called Dongo, where Mussolini was captured and shot. Dongo is pretty, but by the time you take the afternoon ferry, the return ferry is returning and there is no way back. Some of the ferry landings, such as Bellagio, were mobbed with people and there was never any information until the last minute, and then the mob panicked and people got trampled and one day a British woman screamed, "Monsters, all of you!," and got separated from her child in the melee while one Sophia Loren look-alike pressed her young son like a sticker against her body and scowled *prego* loudly, and stepped aside with an elaborate bow to a rambunctious older Rumpelstiltskin of a woman shoving everyone out of her way with a toothless grin.

This is the country that houses the Vatican, the epicenter of Catholicism. This is the home of Mussolini and of the poet Pier Paolo Pasolini, whose movie *Salò, or the 120 Days of Sodom*, I happened upon late one night in my twenties, and, clueless and captivated, I watched the whole thing. I was traumatized for weeks. True, it was based on the namesake book by the French Marquis de Sade, that nut, but those mid-forties Fascists who tortured those eighteen teenagers, I felt they were still alive and probably in that mob with us. The mob had gathered, waited, and congealed for an hour and a half until we all sat there on the landing pier pressed together in our Inferno, even though if you just turned around and gazed at the shiny white yachts sitting on the lake it was heavenly. There was also the persistent fear that you would miss the ferry or that it just wouldn't come and you'd be sleeping on the sand because the last ferry left at the same time as the last bus. Timing became claustrophobic, sort of like the riddle of which days to take sumatriptan, the migraine-abortive medication, when you have daily migraines of varying percentages and you have eight pill days allowed per month. That's why we never took the last ferry.

Eventually, Jerry and I fixed things and I wondered yet again if I was bipolar or if it was the jet lag or prednisone or migraines or menopause, I couldn't separate one from the other anymore. This was aging. It was boiling for the first time in the Lake District's history. The ferries were ovens. Restaurants served pizza. The rich Fascists smoked. A bat flew into the house. The one place we found to eat, usually perch, the waitress cheerfully called us *vicini vicini* (close neighbors) because we wanted to sit next to one another instead of facing one another. The frescoes of angels and the dead Christs hanging everywhere consoled me. At some point, perhaps in the tiny commune of Varenna, we fell back in love, and Jerry took care of me in a way that made me think we could grow old together. It was in Varenna that we found three churches that told a thousand-year story—from the simple medieval stonework and frescoes of Saint John the Baptist to the paintings of hard-suffering saints placed symmetrically around a rococo altarpiece.

Getting back to the migraines. Being on edge all the time is not good for me, and I have no idea if the substitute dog walker will steal something. Any tech-savvy person will eventually gain access to my bank accounts and there are three laptops in the house. I hate having a password on mine. I want the freedom of not having to type in a password every time I get an idea or want to access my repository of ideas. It makes me feel as if I am the criminal. I have already protected my home with cast-iron gates on every window, specialized locks that are unpickable, and metal plates that make doors un-pryable. You cannot break your way in. But your subs can sashay right in and scoop up loot: computers, tchotchkes, underwear, or my mother's chunky purple ring, for which I have no receipt. I want trustworthy people. It is unacceptable to put a client on edge like this every day.

For others, the stress of a substitute dog walker daily may be minor, but for me it is not. Chronic stress increases your stroke risk fourfold, according to the *Journal of Neurology, Neurosurgery, and Psychiatry*. Unlike many other migraine sufferers, I have chronic daily migraines, so it's not a matter of simply popping a sumatriptan. Each day you take it increases your stroke risk. Each migraine day is also a stroke risk day. Basically life has become one giant stroke waiting to fell you once you hit fifty, and suddenly you are looking for a hospital on every corner, measuring your heart rate, wondering if you should go to the emergency room or whether it would waste an evening—or is that stupid because would you waste your life instead by worrying about whether you might waste your evening? This is what it feels like to be old. This is what it feels like to be my dad after all his strokes. This is what it must have felt like to be my mother, waiting for her heart transplant. "They're going to slice my chest open and cut my heart out, Diane," she said starkly, years ago. The concept is terrifying but accurate. That is what it feels like to be old and to entrust your life to medicine and hospitals and worry that you are running out of options but still you hope for the best.

I want to know who will take care of me. My father who has had many strokes and who fell on the street recently because he couldn't lift his foot properly offered to come over and sit with me because of the pain I'm in. Do you have a father like that? He is a physician. He had to look up a condition I have: patulous Eustachian tube dysfunction. My last ENT didn't diagnose it all year. I can't remember how long it has been exactly, because the Topamax has wiped out my memory. It's when your Eustachian tubes are always open and you feel like Darth Vader because your own voice resonates loudly inside your ear, a condition that's called autophonia, and the related pain feels like stinging wind whipping into one ear and out the other. Talking hurts. It's torture to have to ask your subs, "Did my dog do number 1 or number 2? Are you the regular walker? Can you fill the water?" They should just tell me. It is unendurable to have a different person in my home, with no certainty for the foreseeable future about who is coming, when they are coming, and whether they are a normal person or insane or a thief. I cannot tolerate that. I would also rather have a woman. Some days I'm zoned out on the couch with a cold washcloth on my face and a stress thermometer hooked to my finger while I do biofeedback with a migraine relaxation app and my body is just sort of out there.

I don't know if you are still reading and I doubt that you will take note of my suggestion. You never responded to my previous email about whether that guy was going to be the regular walker. I have no objection to the service technically, I only object to your low standards. But I can't go to sleep properly each night (and I must) if I am stressed out about anything at all. If something upsets me enough to keep me up, I cut out of my life the next day. I'm tired of watching people get away with indecent behavior toward other people. People should be held accountable for services that create suffering or pain. I hired you as part of a solution to mitigate my pain and instead you increased it. I don't believe in forgiveness but I do believe in camaraderie because it loosens the noose of loneliness, and believe me, it's tight lately.

When my estrogen dropped, my life changed in five minutes. When you have a stroke, or your organs shut down as you go septic, everything changes in an instant. When you get a call to cut out your heart, everything changes in an instant. It turns out that I plummeted from my last period straight to menopause; it did not happen slowly. My mother never got the transplant. Something happened to the heart that night when she got to Yale New Haven Hospital and while she was nervously waiting they said go home. Thirteen years later, my father went septic at midnight, hours after being released from the hospital after recovering from his last stroke, and I woke up the next morning to dozens of texts and phone messages from my sister and ex-husband on the day of my son's birthday party, and made my way to Cornell Medical Hospital, where my sister was born and my mother had died, to find that my father had made it through the night. He knew he was on borrowed time. So I asked him the questions I hadn't asked my mother: "What does it feel like to know you're about to die? Do you have any regrets?" He had a hard time answering and started crying. I almost-cry a lot and try not to because it gives me a migraine. As I mentioned, the stress of the migraines and the new dog and the new consulting job have been overwhelming.

A substitute dog walker is never going to take into consideration the heightened worries of an owner with a chronic illness. Will this person forget to write down if my dog peed? Who will clean the carpets when that happens and my dog pees on the rug two hours later? I already titrated down one dose on my Topamax because I've lost ten pounds, which is why I needed the dog walker. The Topamax has given me a severe stutter, along with Alzheimer's-like symptoms, stroke-like symptoms (speech is difficult, but writing is lucid), and often I forget what I'm doing in the middle of doing it. I can't keep track of the pee. If she pees, I will have to scrub the carpet five times, and then soak the carpet again with enzymatic cleaner. It is labor-intensive. I'm hypoglycemic and I have extremely low blood pressure (90/60), so leaning over makes me dizzy and the throbbing feeling in my head thumps its way into the first stages of a migraine. I'm iron-deficient, and until the iron infusions are finished, which takes a month, leaning over and scrubbing pee out of the rug will tense up the already knotted muscles in my neck. I can barely hold my head up, and neck spasms cause migraines, too. Our dog clearly has hound in her, or was kept in a basement in Miami, because the squirrels make her like Ahab going after his whale. She pulls so hard on the leash that I worry she will yank my arm out of its socket. That's why I hired you to help me. You are in the service industry. This should be your motto: "Easy dog walking, nice safe people."

This point about accountability is critical if you continue to conduct your business in this leafy family neighborhood that is Park Slope. An airplane crashed here once—did you even know that? I have a complicated relationship with the neighborhood since my divorce. There is quiet wreckage below our feet. This whole place is a cemetery. My mother grew up a few miles over, in Crown Heights. She liked dogs. Her sheltie was named Alex. She wouldn't've liked the way you're handling yourself and she would've typed a letter to the Better Business Bureau on her manual typewriter and then sued you.

I guess you figure there are so many families here, so many potential married clients with children and puppies, that it is fine to be sloppy. Park Slope has so many married people that it's an outlier of a community in the U.S. population per Pew Research, and I think that's because of all the whiteness and therapy and desperation to stay together for the children even though the children see the icy misery first. When you ask people how their vacation was and they always say "Amazing!" as if the world is one giant Like button, you start to wonder: is it you, or is it vacation, or is it people? I get tired of asking people about their vacations. I tell people the truth. I have a secret wish to write a story in which all the people on my wide leafy street get divorced one by one and panic ensues. It turns out to be the PTA cookies, and it's a scourge—as in José Saramago's *Blindness*—and soon the supermarkets are empty and the real estate prices are dropping but people are happier and they are having more sex, and suddenly in school there is more recess.

I got sidetracked. My endocrinologist noticed it, too, the other day. It's Topamax, not your personality, she assured me. I've lost weight. I haven't been 105 pounds since ninth grade, and my son told me I look like a cancer patient. (I should be at least 120 pounds because my thyroid has slowed down considerably, so I should be sleeping nine hours but I'm all amped up and I've had to triple my Klonopin. It's the stress of your unpredictable service.)

Let me tell you a story about accountability. There's a woman who until last week worked at a cheese shop. I met her after my friend Minna Zallman Proctor's book launch for *Landslide: True Stories* at Emma Straub's Books Are Magic bookstore. I wanted everything to go smoothly for Minna's reading. I brought my portable single-use plastic cold pack and had Jerry massage the crystals quietly to make it icy, and I had two liters of cold water and two hundred milligrams of sumatriptan in case I got a migraine. I was prepared. I'd eaten a lot. I put the cold pack on the back of my neck. I hoped her reading would last exactly forty minutes, at which point the cold pack would warm. I ate two shortbread cookies. You can't skip meals if you're a migraine sufferer.

Her reading was vividly eloquent and at one point I almost cried because she wrote about her mother with such tenderness: "How the light caught the soft cut of her cheekbones and her tall forehead, her startling blue eyes, so often diverted because she was shy." Her kids were there and not really listening but I felt glittery, feeling her mother suddenly come alive, the way dead mothers do while you live with them privately in your mind. Her mother smelled like water and pencil shavings, she said precisely. It was beautiful, and coincidentally Minna is beautiful with her Goldilocks hair scrolling down and her Italian gestures (she was partly raised in Tuscany because of her bohemian mother), so it mattered that I went and saw her in her element. I gave her my shiny new earrings for the event.

I noticed for the first time not only her storytelling but the musical rhythm of her prose, the way she stitched sentences together with a poet's pacing. I suppose that came from her mother, a composer, and that's just in her. There were twists and lifts within the language, and that made sense to me as a poet but even more so now—with all the commotion in my brain, the inside of my head is a misshapen place.

I am in menopause. I'm impatient, intolerant, and I have no qualms about saying or doing anything. I use my flaws wisely, like Margaret in *A Wrinkle in Time*. So: I felt a headache building as my ice pack warmed and I bolted, while people were clapping, to find some cold water. Jerry chased me. I dumped my sweater in his arms as a hot flash overwhelmed me. I saw a cheese shop. I grabbed two bottles of water, one to use as an ice pack for my face immediately and one to drink from. A thin, mousy-haired thirtyish woman stood behind the cheese and crostini. I asked her what kind of crostini they were, because they were tinted different colors. "Crostini," she said in a computerized voice designed to resemble a woman's. I looked up, surprised. Usually, I'm not patient. A friend told me that as a migraine sufferer I have to avoid anger, so I make every effort to do so. "Well," I said, "but they are different colors. They must be different." She looked at them. "One's raisin," she conceded, irritated. I grimaced. "Oh. Okay. I'll take one. And I'd like to buy these." I held the bottles up and looked for the register. "Over there," she said, and tossed her head in the direction of the interior, a vast empty space. I wandered into the middle of the store and looked around. "Over there," she repeated. I moved closer to nowhere. It felt like that game of Hot and Cold. "Over there." She must enjoy making people feel discombobulated. The power, the feeling of others' vulnerability. Finally, she appeared by some butcher's block table. She was annoyed, and I tried not to say anything because everything seemed to annoy her. But a few more interactions of disinterest and dislike happened. I stayed calm. I handed her the money. She said to us, in a hard voice, "The doughnuts are free." I smiled. "Not for me." (I'm prediabetic. My A1C and cholesterol are high probably because of all the triple-fat cheese and butter I'm eating to keep my weight up.)

Jerry was interested. I looked at this lady and wondered what kind of person was so rude. Like you, she was in the service industry.

"What kind of doughnut is this one?" asked Jerry. He pointed to one that was passionately sprinkled with nuts but it wasn't clear what was in the middle and there was no hole. She said with disgust, "A doughnut." Anxious, he said, "But it looks like there's something in the middle." Her response, ruder and louder, "So don't take it!" Now I was getting irritated. Jerry is so nice about my migraines, and my panic attacks, and has to handle all my confusion with my medication and my inability to count numbers. He's a trooper and a nice guy. He just wanted a doughnut, and he was there to help me. He's from Texas, and he has a Southern Gothic background. "But no, I mean, it looks like there's something inside, doesn't it?" he said, wounded. I nudged him, *Give up*. He thought he'd said something wrong, that it was his fault. But she was the mean one. I'd had enough. "What's the name of this store?" I asked, though I knew it already. It was Stinky Cheese, and it was previously located in a store that was no larger than a half-bathroom, but now, evidently, occupied this larger space. She didn't answer me and with silent hostility she refused to meet my eyes. I stood there calmly, sort of like a bird of prey. I was much older than her, but I'm told I look much younger, so I presumed that she assumed that I was probably her age. Which means she assumed that we were evenly matched. I was going to use the flaw and talent that I'd inherited from my mother, who could be searing. I tilted my head to the side sweetly. "How much is it?" I asked. "One minute! $4.52," she said. I handed her the money. She handed me my change. I tucked it in my wallet, folded it, slipped it in my bag and looked up. "You know what?" I said. "You're a real fucking cunt."

There was more. She said "karma dharma" and shooed me away, unaware that I was Indian and I understood karma on a deeper level. It's a religious concept, not a rhyme. What she didn't get was that she had it coming, not me. All I was doing was holding her accountable. In retrospect, she's exactly the kind of lady who goes to yoga and says *Om* and does the cultural-appropriation things that I hate. These two Sanskrit words don't go together. They span different religions and concepts. I called her a cunt a bunch of times more, pointed out that she was alone for a reason, that this is how she treats customers, and so on. There was some adrenaline. "Did I do something wrong?" Jerry asked. "People should be held accountable, especially young women," I snapped, holding the water bottle to my head. He checked on Yelp as soon as we got home. "It's not just us!" he yelled. A lot of people had left that store stunned and angry. The next day I spoke to the owner. I told him everything, including the cunt part. We talked about customer service and all the cheese people and chefs we knew in common. That lady got fired.

So you see, when you're in the service industry, the goal is to be invisible to the people you're serving because you are selling simplicity, not stress. Anyway, I got my new prescription with the right amount of Topamax. (I mentioned above that I was dosing down. The secretaries at the neurologist's office were calling in the wrong prescription for two days, and I was having panic attacks that I'd have to go from 75 milligrams to 0 milligrams and basically that would give me an aneurysm or some other fucked-up brain thing because you have to do it 25 milligrams at a time. But my doctor saw my messages and fixed it.) The number-one rule of customer service is "Remember the wow." I'm in consulting. You should have apologized the first time when we called about the ten minutes that the lady skimmed off the walk on day 2.

Clearly you are not a people person. This is my diagnosis of you. I am holding you accountable and ending my relationship with your service. I want my two sets of keys immediately. If I don't receive the keys by the end of the day, I will call the police because then you will have introduced a safety issue.

Sincerely,
Diane Mehta

Secrets of My Mother's Cemetery

We all have a shared history with our family and it has, literally and figuratively, a plot. On the surface, the history of each life—and each death—seems fixed, but like history itself, investigated with a new lens, everything is very much in flux. Neither are circumstances finite. You look at the paper trail of curated information: birth and death certificates; marriage licenses; family trees; diplomas and college degrees; letters; diaries; scrapbooks; bank statements; immigration documents; and photographs of vacations, births, and graduations. But in the moments before and after the photographs, behind the facts, there are true stories worth looking into.

I am middle-aged, so it is inevitable that I'd look back on my experiences to help me understand the future. It is also true that wandering around in cemeteries forces me to wrestle with all the possibilities that my life has left to offer. There's as much variety to cemeteries I've visited as there is variety of experience: London's overgrown Harrow on the Hill, with soft moss creeping up slanted, buck-toothed tombstones; the tiny cemetery on a ridge in the Perugian town of Umbertide, with tributes to citizens that Fascists killed; the Montmartre cemetery in Paris, with dusty, crowded Jewish tombstones on which are carved long lists of bodiless people murdered by the Nazis; and my local Green-Wood Cemetery, on Brooklyn's highest hill, outfitted with benches and a little lake and the cheerful expectation that people will visit and picnic.

Cemeteries are grounded in centuries of history and people's contributions to it. I can disappear for hours in cemeteries, losing myself in strangers' families and lives, instead of my own. I want to believe that the knowledge we seek about our ancestors and ourselves is eternally being worked out, like a laboratory experiment that fuses generations and generates a cumulative imagination. Cemeteries hold hundreds of millions of secrets, forever opaque to the living: glass that grows, ears with singing still in them, melodies composed but never scored, parents we didn't know, unsolved murders, deeds to stolen property, families who had slaves, men who sold their daughters, women who had affairs, and children who no one wanted to claim as theirs. Cemeteries are places that feel quietly theatrical because they belong not to us but to the dead.

We cannot measure what goes on in cemeteries any more than our instruments can measure what truly goes on in space. Dark matter is incomprehensible except as something inferred: it has a gravitational effect on visible matter, but we don't know what it is. Similarly, the dead exert their gravity on us in that we cannot let them go. The dead may not care about us any longer—and I'm not sure they should. Reasonable people spend much of their lives trying to figure out how to be properly alive while they are in possession of what it means to be properly dead, and I doubt that either group envies the other.

Delmore Schwartz's epic poem *Genesis I and II*, about the childhood of a young Jewish boy named Hershey Green whose grandparents immigrated from Europe and whose parents are miserable, alternates between a chorus of ghosts (cranky older Jewish men) in verse and a prose-like narrative about the lives of two families whose children marry. This freshly dead ghost immediately smiles because he is savvy to the fact that life is just a show:

> When I looked down at Life for the first time,
> It was as if I turned to the comic strips,
> And lit a cigarette for the first time,
> And in deep relaxation, started slowly
> To smile, then roared! at the mere black-and-white
> Unlikely slots and strips of comedy,
> Speaking balloons!

Then the ghost gets a little sad because, well, life is just a show:

> And several of the older dead nearby
> Suggested that I look at the starry sky
> Above this life, the moral law within

If we are taken aback when faced with the idea that life is theater, it is only because we have failed to recognize that who we are and how we live is only the prelude to who we want to become and how we hope to live. Even if there is no meaning of life, it does not mean that you cannot have a meaningful life.

Writing in a letter to his son, who he expects will not read the letter until he is an adult, the terminally ill pastor in Marilynne Robinson's *Gilead* imagines becoming an expert at being dead: "I'll know most of what there is to know about being dead, but I'll probably keep it to myself." The human act of knowing, while dead, is a wry leap of faith. It makes death less macabre to think that we can accrue expertise in it, as if the dead had their own style of living.

The first time I visited Green-Wood Cemetery in Brooklyn, I was a newly divorced single parent in middle age who didn't have a wonderful grip on reality. My mother had been dead since I was thirty-five and although my father had emerged astonishingly intact from all of his strokes, I knew eventually he would not survive. I'd become at ease in hospitals, efficient at managing the procedures of medical care, and versed in the language of illness, the dying, and the dead. The clock ticked faster. My father's years were fleeing fast and mine were starting to look a little abbreviated. When I began writing my novel, it was probably a way to look more closely at my parents' lives and their unhappiness instead of my own. I would get to the heart of their miserable marriage and what it did to me! The novel would be ugly, to show what it was like to be my mother: to be Jewish and pathologically smart, angry, overlooked, and die, in that order. I'd dramatize the story of my father, whose Jainism shaped his moral center but left him emotionally remote. There would be romance, but it wouldn't be between my parents. In one draft I made the mother character kill herself, and in the next I gave my fictional parents a happy future, together. I wanted more love in my future, from them and from others. I was convinced that I would never lead a full life without figuring them out. Eventually I made my fictional parents separate and get back together.

Graham Greene recognized that all stories are interior: "A story has no beginning or end: arbitrarily one chooses that moment of experience from which to look back or from which to look ahead." In this story of my parents, I move around the pieces and reframe their destinies in no particular order. It does not feel important for their story to be true, only for me to chase the story. Maria Stepanova's book *In Memory of Memory* is about her effort to pin down her family history. She begins with a parable about finding her great-grandfather's home in Russia—she recognizes everything and feels great about the discovery, but it turns out it was someone else's home. There was never anything to hold onto but memory.

It doesn't matter which cemetery you go to, because the dead members of your family are not on Earth but in your memory. I have not visited my mother's grave in more than twenty years, but I have thought about it a great deal. It is in New Jersey, and there is no way of getting there conveniently except by renting a car, and then there would be all that driving just to cry—or maybe not to cry—and return home pretending that my mother had seen me. We all like movie scenes in which the protagonist goes to the grave of their loved one and lies there or weeps. It is a romantic story. The flowers we bring die, just like they did, and then we leave, just like they did.

Green-Wood was as good a place as any to vaguely feel as if I was going to my mother's cemetery. From the perspective of convenience, all I ever needed was an aura of a place and a recognition that my mother was dead—I did not need to be near the skeleton itself. I wanted to take a walk in a park. Green-Wood was founded in 1838 and it was one of the first rural cemeteries that came out of the English school of "landscape gardening"—as a reaction to the "rigid geometries" of French neoclassical design, says historian Thomas Campanella. Rural cemeteries offered "studied informality" and a facsimile of the chaos of nature instead. (The first rural cemetery was Père Lachaise in Paris, founded in 1804.) Green-Wood, says Campanella, was "thronged from the start." Everyone in Paris and New York was promenading in these parks that doubled as cemeteries—people loved it. They still do: Green-Wood's wooded-glen landscape is a lovely place to spend an afternoon, especially if you are not in mourning.

The first time I visited Green-Wood, I hoped I'd find homespun tales of turn-of-the-century Brooklyn Jewish families, like the one my mother grew up in. I was surprised by the grand neo-Gothic entrance, and marveled at the hills to the left, lake to the right, and healthy green grass everywhere. I veered left up a steep hill before descending into a woodsy area where angels leaned over stone caskets or posed on plinths. They had Pre-Raphaelite hair that curled eternally and tall, muscular wings poised powerfully behind them as if reminding us that they could just fly off. I'd been binge-watching *Doctor Who* with my son, and they reminded me of the Weeping Angels on the show—predatory creatures that sweep you back in time to steal the life you've already lived. If you turned away or blinked, the angels were immediately upon you. It was a brilliant dramatic device for a sci-fi television show and a profound way of urging viewers to feel the urgency of their time on Earth. The actual stone angels in the cemetery were there to protect the dead. But it is we, the living, who need protecting, not from death but from not properly living.

I'll get what I want! you think when you are in your twenties. "Youth is like having a big plate of candy," said F. Scott Fitzgerald. I wanted to be known for having verbal fireworks in my poems but I did not pause to think about philosophy. I wanted to find a handsome, rugged lover with a svelte way of thinking, but the visage always took over. I wanted to see myself as a beautiful woman instead of the ugly girl in grade school, but I did not take seriously the few people who signaled romantic interest. I wanted to live a radical and unusual life enlivened by literature and with much adventure, but I never put myself in danger.

Twenty years later, I realized that I hadn't published enough, and though I'd shifted my career to raise my son, I found parenting a young child laborious and intellectually unsatisfying. I wanted to work and I didn't feel loved. I wasn't sure if I'd accomplished anything except giving birth and writing a bunch of poems and articles. But maybe it's only when we have exited a time in which we were not really living that we figure out how to.

"I went to the woods because I wished to live deliberately, to front only the essential facts of life, and see if I could not learn what it had to teach, and not, when I came to die, discover that I had not lived," said Henry David Thoreau. He had decided that contentment, or some version of it, was interior instead of material. Thoreau was twenty-eight years old in 1845, when he went to live at Walden Pond. He died of tuberculosis at forty-five, which for our generation is the beginning of middle age. Walden Pond was an awakening, especially for a transcendentalist like Thoreau, who believed that he would find divinity in nature. Here is Thoreau on his afternoon rambles and the passing of shadows on the ground:

> I stood in the very abutment of a rainbow's arch, which filled the lower stratum of the atmosphere, tingeing the grass and leaves around, and dazzling me as if I looked through colored crystal. It was a lake of rainbow light, in which, for a short while, I lived like a dolphin.

He was doing nothing but was actively doing—he was noticing things. He didn't see a rainbow but he entered it, and embodied the life of a dolphin. "Simplicity, simplicity, simplicity!" Thoreau advised. You do not have to look for (or find) the meaning of life; you only have to experience it.

During our uneasy march into the future, we make observations about ourselves. Looking around the scene at Green-Wood, I stared with horrified fascination at the private mausoleums in which wealthy families chose to be buried. Waste of money, my child-of-the-Depression mother would have said. Socioeconomic inequities are in evidence everywhere, but they do not follow us to our graves. (Dead is dead.) The mansions made of marble are designed for the dying and for the relatives who visit. It is our vanity that compels us to build fortresses for our bones in a park swarming with dead souls and visitors picnicking while blue skies swirl overhead and the ground churns with maggots, worms, and human cells. So much pomp! And each gravestone sums up, proudly and with certitude, a life boiled down to one thing: Ida was a good mother, Stan was a good earner.

When we meet people, we always ask what they do. And while it is true that what we do defines us, it also restricts us. I decided to change the story of Ida and Stan. Ida was not a good mother, but her gaze was a thunderbolt and she wanted to be a statistician. Math for her was a spider web she was forever unspooling. Tired of working at the docks, Stan wanted to be a photographer. My story was not better or worse than what was written on their tombstones. Maybe the boiled versions were true. I fretted: Would I, too, be distilled to an aphorism? Ugly immigrant came to mind, the story of my childhood, or overly passionate malcontent writer. Better to have nothing, or a quote. I looked around for simple gravestones that listed only the years lived, and which left possibilities to the imagination. Those were more satisfying. This man, musical prodigy, was composing a jazz sonata in his head when he was knifed on his front steps. This woman created the science of home economics and loved to climb mountains. Here is a marine, killed days after the Battle of Belleau Wood began, during that first American entry into World War I. It is because of men like him that the tide turned against the Germans. Down the slope is a man who spent his life in and out of a federal prison, after a childhood in foster care. His mother, a drunk, was thrown in an asylum when his baby sister was discovered dead from neglect. His father was stationed somewhere. Back to what Graham Greene said: "A story has no beginning or end: arbitrarily one chooses that moment of experience from which to look back or from which to look ahead."

My mother is buried in a section of a Jewish cemetery in Clifton, New Jersey, called King Solomon Memorial Park. Her bones fill her dress under a wide-canopied tree. She was a wife and mother, her tombstone says, overlooking her quantity of feeling, and the things she taught me.

After we moved to the States, in 1973, my mother went about giving my sister and me a proper education. My father, a physician, was expert at understanding the mechanics of the body, and she was skilled at contemplating art and ideas. She wanted us to be critical people, to have opinions. Our mother quizzed us on paintings at the Metropolitan Museum of Art in New York; we were expected to identify a Rembrandt and a Monet, among others. To do this, we diligently observed the white-lace frilly collars that reflected light on the faces of Rembrandt's subjects and recognized the pointillist diffusion of outdoor light in Monet's landscapes. I must have been thirteen then. It was because of her that I understood the grown-up secret of what conducting was, too, and hewed to loud, dramatic approaches. She loved the flamboyant, breathless conducting styles of Leonard Bernstein and Zubin Mehta, the former expressive and the latter violent in their gestures. They were men of bold interpretations and grand, arm-flinging feelings. She loved the big feelings, I realize now, because they took her out of everything that felt ordinary.

My mother took us to see Thornton Wilder's Pulitzer Prize–winning play *Our Town* several times. It's a universal story about an ordinary couple in the fictional town of Grover's Corners, New Hampshire, in the early 1900s. The play clearly struck a chord in my mother, but it has taken me much of my life to figure out why. "We like the sun comin' up over the mountain in the morning, and we all notice a good deal about the birds," says one of the residents in Grover's Corners. They live out their lives without too much introspection. Their cultural references are simple: they know *Robinson Crusoe* and the Bible, Handel's Largo, and *Whistler's Mother*. The drama probes nothing less than the meaning of life, and it comes up empty. *Our Town* is about regret. It was clear that my mother, even in middle age, regretted her inability to live her life more fully. She was probably my age when we saw *Our Town*, back then. It must have been so exciting to meet a handsome Indian man and marry him, then go to India and raise two children there—and how terrifying it must have been to unravel, to check into a hospital, and to wonder if she would ever be okay. It startles me to remember her still.

Once my parents left India, my mother's life was no less domestic and ordinary than the women in Grover's Corners, cooking four decades of meals for their husbands and eating those meals in five minutes. I wonder at what point she swerved from a woman of intellectual exuberance into a despondent housewife who had so little, and who told me that the radio saved her life. Could she have known that her children, and a handful of articles, letters, recipes, and conversations, would be the sum total of her output? Her enlarged heart began failing in her sixties and she was put on the heart transplant list at Yale New Haven Hospital—she and my father lived in Connecticut at the time. But eventually, after many ICU wards and step-down facilities, and several psych wards and many diseases later, she was removed from the list and calmly reconciled herself to the fact that her possibilities had vanished. She hadn't done much with her enormous talents. She had underestimated herself. Finally, just like the residents of Grover's Corners, there was no more angling for anything deeper, she was simply living. "Do you want to have children?" she asked me before she died, and pointed out that she will never meet them.

When *Our Town*'s protagonist Emily Webb dies in childbirth, she begs the dead who are attending her funeral to relive a moment in her life. Sensing how it will end up, they insist that Emily select an unimportant day. Emily picks her twelfth birthday.

> I can't bear it. They're so young and beautiful. Why did they ever have to get old? Mama, I'm here. I'm grown up. I love you all, everything.—I can't look at everything hard enough.

Delight turns to despair: Emily is pained by how little attention the living pay to the significance of each moment. "To move about in a cloud of ignorance"—that's what living is. It introduces the riddle of what fulfillment is. Back to Thoreau: "I went to the woods because I wished to live deliberately, to front only the essential facts of life, and see if I could not learn what it had to teach, and not, when I came to die, discover that I had not lived."

Indians have always checked their fortunes before marriage, seeking guarantees for fulfillment. My father was one of three out of six children in his family to choose a love marriage over an arranged one. While I was writing my novel, I hired an astrologer in India to tell me my father's horoscope even though he has already lived most of his life. The astrologer gave me specific dates for fortunate or unfortunate days or years, and, based on my father's birth date and time, culled insights into my dad's personality and marriage. He said my father was a man whose truths should be taken with a 30 to 40 percent discount, and that he had a roving eye. The entire horoscope was amusingly false, except that my father's marriage was destined to be difficult. The truth is that my mother crushed him with her contempt and her pathologies, and he drained her love with his indifference. Would it have changed anything if my father had received this warning before he married my mother? What would she have done if she had known how things would work out?

Burdened with foresight, we'd have no free will, no serendipity. We'd just be good at everything, like Bill Murray in *Groundhog Day*. We would never conduct ourselves abominably, or ask for forgiveness, and we would be successful and love our spouses and children the way they want to be loved. But we would not be curious enough to try things. The burden of knowledge would make the days unbearable.

> If you should dip your hand in,
> your wrist would ache immediately,
> your bones would begin to ache and your hand would burn
> as if the water were a transmutation of fire
> that feeds on stones and burns with a dark gray flame.

Elizabeth Bishop's "At the Fishhouses" resonates because knowledge has pain built into it. With pain comes humility about what to do with your tiny place on Earth and how to get more constancies of joy than suffering.

My second time at Green-Wood, I came across an idyllic lake surrounded by shady trees that reflected back upon themselves, with benches set up on the slope for contemplation. But I think of cemeteries as noisy places because of all the conversations going on below the surface. It felt good to imagine my mother here, chatting with other Brooklyn-born Jews about their experiences. Bernard Malamud's luckless grocer Morris Bober, in *The Assistant*, was looking for people who appreciated his talent for finely slicing meats. "Why so sad, skin-and-bones, eat, eat?" he'd say and gaze at his cashless drawer while frowning at the rich shop owner across the street with two franchises. My mother would shake her head at this and say that with Morris it wasn't about the meats but about the pleasure of talking to customers: the Swedish painter who came for beer, the Italian girl who wanted ham. My mother had a knack for seeing things with more reality than they appeared.

Perhaps this is why my mother destroyed as much as possible before she died—to keep us from seeing the nature of her jagged feelings. But what's left is a trove: an archive of letters to her parents from her first trip to Europe. Not long after her funeral, my father photocopied those letters and gave my sister and I our mother's fifty pages of wild feelings. The way she narrated her travels was eloquent for a woman of eighteen, and showed me how the world, and foreign men, were beginning to open up to her. When I read the letters, I am right there with her in Nice, Rome, islands off the coast of Sweden. What will the pastor's son in *Gilead* feel when he reads that letter from his long-dead father? I'm not sure which are more concrete: his memories of his father or his father's memories of him, detailed in the letters.

We are eager to collect experience to ensure that we will not end up with an ordinary job in an ordinary town with an ordinary spouse. But happiness does not arrive in the usual ways.

Give me the secret, I say vaguely to the cemeteries. "Play your part!" someone screams. A young girl delivers a sermon and an older man weaves together the remnants of exploding galaxies on a nineteenth-century spinning wheel. Ears and noses fall from the sky and the theory of everything in the physical universe explains its framework. Someone writes a couplet. Ordinary spirits laugh but it sounds like owls. "I thought you were going to be a window dresser," my mother yells from New Jersey.

Married, with Turtle

Dear Angus:

We set you free between the pregnancy and the wedding. You are a red-eared slider turtle with a foster-child past. You were named after Angus, a middle-schooler with long hair whose parents adopted you from a pet store in Williamsburg or South Brooklyn. Angus's father remodeled choppers and looked like he'd just come out of a *Mad Max* movie; he wore patent leather platform boots and carried a walking stick with a skull for a handle, and Angus's mom was a female version of the dad. "They looked like they were at a heavy metal costume party at all times," said my ex-husband Tom, who inherited you from Angus's parents the year before we started dating.

People never know what they're getting into when they buy a turtle. We think we will teach our children empathy by encouraging them to care for a living being who is more vulnerable than they are, but I wonder if this experiment makes a child more vulnerable yet. It must feel good, when you are young, to realize that you can love someone who is not your parents. By sharing his name with you, Angus probably thought that he had secured your place in the family. From the perspective of a child, home and everything in it is fixed. If you have a turtle, you will always have a turtle.

Every family has its rituals. If your family was like mine, your weekday probably went like this: Angus ran home from school and hoisted you in the air, and while you pumped your legs, hoping to reach water or solid ground, he carried you to the backyard, put you on the grass, and watched in amazement as your head slowly emerged from its carapace. You scuttled around the fenced-in yard and investigated a puddle, searched for snails, or climbed onto a rock to bask in the sun. Angus kicked a ball and chased it. Angus's father revved the motorcycle he was fixing in the driveway.

Angus reached an age when families separate. His father found a new wife who resembled Anna Nicole Smith, with platinum hair and glossy bangs that erupted from a thin brown streak on her scalp. She and Angus's dad shared a love of tattoos and were visually compatible, and his Kerouac vibe complemented her centerfold-y air. She'd briefly worked as a stripper at The Glass Slipper in Boston, a dive bar with one pole, and had befriended my ex-husband when she became a department assistant at the publishing company where he worked, and still works. You continued to live with Angus and his dad, who married his girlfriend, and Angus's free-spirited mother attended the wedding with the bass player from Weezer. Angus's dad and the bride took Angus-the-child and moved out West.

You were as big as the diameter of a tea saucer when Tom adopted you. He lived alone in a second-floor railroad apartment in a Brooklyn brownstone near Flatbush Avenue. You loved being in the bathtub or taking a jog around the apartment while he cleaned the tank. He was always there for you, except the time he left town for a long weekend and couldn't find anyone to feed you or change the water in your tank, but he filled up the bathtub and threw in plenty of turtle food flakes and it was fine.

While writing this essay, I learned a little about red-eared slider turtles. Their shells are composed of fused ribs divided into scutes, which absorb vitamin D to grow bone. They don't have nostrils but smell through nerves on bumps under the chin called "barbels." Prospect Park was a short walk from Tom's apartment, so when the window was open, you probably smelled the musky coats of skunks and raccoons, feral cats with kidney disease, feathers shed by birds winging by on the Atlantic Flyway, dried leaves, and tree blossoms.

Red-eared sliders come from the Mississippi River and the Gulf of Mexico, and are bred industrially for the pet trade. Sliders are exported all over the world. Fifty-two million of them were sent out for export between 1989 and 1997. According to the Global Invasive

Species Database, sliders destroy the indigenous ecosystems they are released into. Don't take this personally! You are not responsible for the ecosystem, the illegal pet trade, or the phenomenon of turtle releases after the Ninja Turtles craze died down, and neither are you the cause of the divorces (Angus's parents, Angus's dad and the bride, Tom and me) or the abortion.

The abortion was necessitated by an extra copy of trisomy 21—not because you carried salmonella. Either my egg was derelict, our sperm-egg unification didn't go well (ominous), or my egg aged out. Not everyone survives in a family, whether they are wanted or not. What is plain from the history of your species is that everyone wanted you: hatchery owners, suppliers, smugglers, banks, money launderers, pet stores, chefs, single people, and parents who want their children to have a pet that offers more interaction than a goldfish and less work than a dog.

I became interested in what happened to you when Tom's new wife got pregnant with his second baby and I couldn't control the story of our family anymore. But there are true stories about families, and there are fictional stories about families.

Your family name is *Trachemys scripta elegans*. You did not come with a birth certificate or tracking number, so I created an origin story. You were born in July with eight other turtles at a hatchery in rural Missouri, and you owe your life to the boom in profits from the illegal turtle trade. Your mother left the nest after she created you, which is a sign of how much she believed in you—a precocious turtle. Every mother has a job: to deliver a child safely and launch them on their way. After you were decontaminated, you were incubated for sixty-five days with hundreds of hatchlings. When you emerged whole from your egg, approximately two inches long, your owners shipped you to a pet store with two dozen other hatchlings in a ventilated cardboard box.

Tom was your third foster parent. We met at the publishing house where he also met the woman who moved out West with Mad Max and Angus. I knew him as the tall, slim guy who worked for an imprint that published language learning guides and test prep books, ran eight miles a day, walked around the halls bobbing his head sideways to indie-rock on his headphones, and lamented that the Red Sox had not won the World Series since 1918. Sometimes he whaled balls at a colleague. He'd been a pitcher in college and he seemed well adjusted and easygoing in a way that I was not.

On our first date, Tom and I met on the Coney Island boardwalk in South Brooklyn. We proceeded to the batting cage (where Tom slugged at fastballs in a sweat), spun above the Atlantic seascape on the Ferris wheel, posed in a photobooth, and walked along the boardwalk in the sun. Coney Island revived memories of going on the maniac, whiplash rides with my sister, accompanied by our maternal grandparents when we were little, and eating cotton candy, which melts the moment your tongue touches the spun sugar. Eating it was a competition between the disappearing candy and my desire to savor the feeling of eating the candy. There are some gifts that families give you without recognizing that it will make a lasting impression. You were one of those gifts.

The first time we met, you darted under the bed and didn't emerge until I stood motionless in the corner for a few minutes. You resembled a rock. Did you have a personality? I wish I knew. The internet says turtles have feelings, but even so, you were already on your third foster home and what are "feelings" for a turtle? Perhaps these feelings are connected to the smell of someone familiar who you rely on for food, or feelings connected to routines, which is how we tend to measure life: I do this, I do that. My ex-husband and I never talked about feelings during our marriage, so I'm not surprised that he is not responding to my emails loaded with questions about you. He says he is busy taking care of his new son, who is a toddler. So I will fill in those early days for you.

Three months after we met, Tom asked me to join him on a bicycle trip across Cambodia. I said yes immediately and canceled my plans to go to Bombay for my cousin's wedding. Cambodia seemed promising. The founder of SpiceRoads, a British guy named Hamish, sent explicit directions about what we'd need and what to expect, but we shrugged it off because we figured we were in good shape. We bought cycling shorts with the loose, contemporary fit of Bermuda shorts and half the padding as the pro shorts. We purchased squeezable water bottles and cycling shoes that did not attach to pedals. Tom asked his neighbor to take care of you, and she agreed to change your water once a week, which seemed pretty reasonable given how heavy the tank was and the fact that you dragged a lot of slime around with you on the carpet. We boarded a plane from New York to LA, transferred to Taipei, and transferred again to Chiang Mai before making our way to Poipet, a honkytonk Thai border town. Everyone who signed up for the cycling tour stayed at the same hotel: a white concrete building with a rooster in the courtyard and an all-night lounge and karaoke room where a woman crooned American standards below our bedroom, which vibrated worryingly and compelled us to request a room change in the middle of the night. The next morning, our group crossed into Cambodia.

We cycled between 70 and 100 kilometers a day for the next 10 days, in triple-digit heat up to 120 degrees—the rains were late and humidity dripped from the leaves and coated our skin. It didn't occur to me that you might have loved the swampy wilderness and the climate, but it's also possible that someone would have scooped you up and eaten you, and it's possible we would have eaten you ourselves because we were so hungry, and the soggy, hygienic, pan-Asian tourist buffets were awful. I popped pills for anxiety, diarrhea, constipation, and muscle pain. We both got heat exhaustion after cycling 48 kilometers on the evening of the first day, from Poipet to Sisophon, or "beautiful lady," a town that was ceded to French Indochina in 1906, and went to Cambodia when it became independent in 1953. Our motel room's air conditioner stalled and screeched, hair clogged the sink, and a rancid smell wafted up from the garbage pail, which appeared to contain puke or human feces. The new room was cleaner. We cranked up the air conditioner, which released a temperate breeze. Tom refused to leave the bed because he was so sick, but I encouraged him to come to dinner and eat white rice. I had not been ready to take care of someone I did not know very well, which is similar to how I felt about you. For a few days, I stopped loving Tom. Not only was he sick, but it was his first trip to Asia and he was wide-eyed and agog at everything, which was not attractive. "You're not a worldly person," he remembers me saying.

There are two kinds of caring: caring you choose because you love someone, and caring that is foisted on you. A lot of rice, bananas, and Imodium helped Tom recover, and he stopped being afraid of being ill in a foreign country and stopped asking if everything was a temple. I don't know if you worried about us, or about yourself; maybe you wondered if you had a new foster parent when the neighbor came in. Anyway, we got used to eating, and burning off, four thousand calories a day. We dragged our bicycles across muddy or flooded terrain up to our waists, bicycled on sand for hours, drank warm water because the supply van had no cooler, slept in guesthouses with showers that trickled water, suffered chafing and groin pain from thinly padded cycling shorts, and shat behind slim trees in open fields while the group looked away and Hamish shouted "stick to the path" to remind us about the land mines.

Ten days on flat roads with increasing distances and difficulty was a buildup to the finale: the thousand-meter-high Bokor Mountain in Kampot, a tranquil city of pepper plantations and a national park. The tour guides were pro cyclers and they were amped. The climb was steep. In a fit of maniac competitiveness, Tom tackled the slope, navigating like a goat over stones and roots, and reached the top first. I bore down on the pedals, off my seat in the lowest gear, and made it halfway before signaling to the van.

Contented, we decided to split with the group one day early, so Hamish drove us to the coastal city of Sihanoukville on the Gulf of Thailand and we spent our last night in hospital beds, in a guesthouse that had once been a hospital. Tom remembers being excited to see the dirt road disappear behind us as we approached Thailand.

Our reward was a weekend on an island in southern Thailand, but the bathroom had an open ceiling that invited mosquitoes to come and go, so the next day we caught a ride to Bangkok and checked into the Imperial Hotel, where we were notified that shorts weren't allowed in the hotel's public spaces and directed to a shopping district. We luxuriated in the neo-colonial room and reveled in the service; our floor had its own concierge and we were so well cared for, which mattered because my mother had died the previous year and the only other place I ever felt cared for was at the Taj in Bombay, one of the most expensive hotels in India.

Back in New York, I went to the doctor to see about my lingering malaise and nausea. He called the next day with news that I was pregnant. I told Tom, and we stared at the air beyond one another's heads, and then he wandered into the living room. I called my sister, who said: "Have it!" The next day, Tom accompanied me to my gynecologist "just to make sure," and the doctor pointed at the sonogram and said I was three months pregnant. We stared at the bean emitting electrical signals that resembled a heartbeat and decided to have it. I was dismayed when the ob-gyn said to stop taking any medication except Tylenol for the remainder of the pregnancy. In the taxi back to the office, Tom asked, "Do you want to get married?" and I said "No, do you?" and he said "No," and that was that.

You and Tom moved into my 950-square-foot one-bedroom apartment in Peter Cooper Village, a 1940s garden development designed to house returning veterans after the war. Metropolitan Life Insurance, which owned the development, promoted country living in an urban landscape; the first tenants moved in August 1, 1947. It was the kind of place where people longed to bring up children.

We put your tank against the wall, beside the wooden dinner table that doubled as my desk. I was not fond of pets, not since my goldfish died in middle school, and having a baby on the way convinced me that pets belonged in their natural habitat and not my house. Men never arrive with just a turtle. The task of cleaning the turtle tank, and caring for the turtle, would fall to me. Organizing a household and keeping a family together always falls to the woman, and people who think that parents share the burden of raising a child and managing a home equally are hallucinating. It requires so much to care for one little human being that you have to quiet any contrary feelings about what you signed up for and believe without question that the family structure is good for the ecosystem.

❧ ❧

It is important for me to tell you that you were the first part of our family, when we were figuring out what a family was. The second part was realizing that we wanted a family. Most people plan their families in the wrong order because things don't always happen in the way they expect.

How exciting it was to be having a department baby in a publishing house full of women. I bought the book *What to Expect When You're Expecting* and followed along. Our colleagues were already revved about the romance, and pregnancy put them over. So it was unfortunate when I got the results of the amniocentesis in my cubicle. The sixteenth floor got quieter as my sobs got louder, and the man who sat diagonal from me on the other side of my cubicle wall asked if I was okay, and then I heard his chair squeak and his footsteps fade. By the time Tom appeared at my cubicle opening five minutes later with his coat on, he looked stricken; our colleagues looked away while we walked across the carpet to the glass double door, and opened it, and the people in the elevator understood that it would be a difficult ride down, which it was, and we left the building.

Maybe you noticed that something had changed during that long weekend before the abortion. I did not realize that I was just at the edge of the second trimester, and that over the weekend I had entered it. When I got to the clinic, they put me in a seesaw contraption with my legs open and swung it up while blood rushed to my head and they explained that because I was so far along, they had to dilate my cervix with seaweed—it would only take a second—and I should return the next day for the abortion. I shook in agony while I put my pants on afterward and Tom looked panicky when he saw my face. They did not give me anesthesia, because junkies also got abortions and they didn't want to hand out pain medication to just anyone, so they told me to take Tylenol.

If you listened, that night, you probably heard screaming. I did not realize that I was in labor. Tom's mother was a retired labor and delivery nurse, and when I told her the bed was wet, she said my water had broken, and that that I should go to the emergency room immediately if I felt like I had to push. "What am I going to tell them?" I yelled at Tom, who was relaying her instructions. "That I had half an abortion?" When you are twenty weeks pregnant, a child is not developed enough to survive outside a womb for more than a few hours. I knew that over the course of the night, at home, the baby had died, and I just wanted it out because I had stopped loving it the evening after getting the news. The baby became a fetus again.

Tom put my legs on his shoulders, the only position that offered a little relief. Then my dad arrived with his painkillers, which were ineffective, and my sister arrived with her Vicodin, which helped, and I called my anesthesiologist cousin to explain that I'd taken all these drugs even though they told me to take only Tylenol. She said just bring the bottles of drugs and then it's the anesthesiologist's problem. That made sense. The next day, I got the abortion part 2, and woke up on a gurney next to a dozen other women on gurneys, and as we grew less groggy we were moved to recliners with our IVs and had cookies while we bled on giant pads that the nurses periodically changed.

On the way out, I stopped at the desk and asked for genetic testing on the fetus, and the secretaries stopped what they were doing and asked which doctor had sent me there. I said the baby had Down syndrome. After they said that they could not do genetic testing, I left the building and struggled to remember whether, in the half-state after the anesthesia started wearing off and before the gurney room, I saw the fetus on a table. Did my anesthesia mind conjure a tiny, reptilian fetus on a metal table or did my psychological mind create a memory of it to concretize the child that might have been, and the feelings that lingered? God, it was like carrying a rock in my body the second I decided to end the pregnancy.

Two months after the abortion, we eloped in Central Park's north woods. Two months after we eloped, we threw a wedding party in a Chinatown loft, catered an Indian buffet, and hoped to get some decent presents. I wore a fitted black evening dress with gold and silver sequins in a geometric pattern—no makeup, and flats. Tom wore his best suit. We didn't talk to one another because we were so busy, and in its way, this prepared us for marriage and parenting. Tom's stripper friend arrived with Mad Max in a beautiful white dress. Later, Tom confessed that she did not think I was good enough for him. Maybe she thought that I had nothing to say because I had never inscribed anything on my body, but I suspect that the real reason was my brown skin, which I did not adorn with cosmetics or tattoos, and maybe I looked poor and dirty—not what she had in mind for Tom's second wife. But other people do not get to decide who becomes your family. I looked her up, and she is a life coach now, with some sort of "life system" she designed to "make your dream life a reality." In her promo video on YouTube, she says of herself, "People call me the original spiritual Type A go-getter."

It's true that we got married because of the abortion, but it is also true that the abortion made plain that I wanted a family. I got pregnant again. There was a lot of vomiting and lethargy, and all I remember was that you smelled like sour wet lettuce and dirt. Tom was ready. He was surprised at how often he had to "fucking clean the tank out," he says now. You can get rid of a turtle a lot more easily than a baby.

We released you on a sandy beach on a sunny day in April. When we examined the map to find you a suitable home, we were surprised. Could it be? Turtle Pond hosted a diverse group of snapping, painted, musk, box, and red-eared sliders, according to the Central Park Conservancy. It would be a continuous party. In the winter, you'd warm yourself on rocks, and in summer you'd loaf about, celebrating "O Nature, your primal sanities!" as Walt Whitman observed. You were ready to launch. It would be the most exciting thing that had ever happened to you. We wanted to believe you'd would be in love with freedom ("O such for me! O an intense life! O full to repletion, and varied!") the way we were in love with the idea of being a family. I fretted that you might have forgotten how to be a turtle, but when we opened your box, you darted into the water as if you had never liked us at all.

Now that I've had three failed pets and one failed pregnancy, I consider how little is sustainable in a family. Tom says your species has a life span of thirty years so you might still be paddling around where we left you, thinking: sky, tree, pond, food, mud. Daylight and seasons crawl over your shell, if you survived, and you probably found a partner or two and have children. As for Tom and me, we went back to our apartment and had a healthy baby one year later, in 2004, the year the Red Sox won the World Series.

Throw Memories into the Wall

A few years ago, Jerry signed us up for a meditation program. I agreed to try it. For two hundred dollars a month, I expected scientifically proven breathing exercises that manage anxiety. Instead, the instructors told me to stare at a silver sticker on the wall in a windowless room. Five inches in circumference, the sticker embodied the "magnetic sun," which was a garbage disposal for memories. The methodology was pared down: You called a memory up and threw it into the sun. Then another, and another. Eventually you start feeling better.

"You're dead," said the guide during my first session. "You've been dead a long time." I started crying. "What do you see?" she asked. I whimpered, "My dad somewhere, cremated, maybe a river, gone for decades. My son is older. He has a family. He thinks of me sometimes. I can't stand it."

"They've been gone a long time. You're fine. Part of the universe. The beginning of what you were meant to be. Does the beanbag chair you don't like matter? What about your job, the argument with your boyfriend, last night's burger? Your dresses, shoes, jewelry, house, keys. Throw your keys away. Throw them into the magnetic sun. Whoosh. Do it again. Whoosh." My mind began to empty. The guide encouraged me to keep throwing things away. "It gets easier. Throw it away. Whoosh. How do you feel?"

I wiped my tears and scanned my imagination. There were countless new dimensions to explore, ways to be and not be, and as soon as I reached out with my arm, a baritone darkness crumpled around me. The cosmic microwave background whispered primordial stories. I thought I saw a neutron star but I was inside it already, and seconds later, I collided with a galaxy and the ripples hummed as if shifting from first to second gear.

Whoosh. Stream-of-consciousness thoughts filled my mind up: a minotaur, a turn in the Penobscot River, the crystal sound of a male cantor singing, my grandmother putting her teeth in and grinning, the moment when the nurse plunked my son on my chest and the tiny being I made gazed at me. I winced and threw it all away.

An optical trick made the sticker more convincing. I'd squint to make the circle blurry and the light flicker. This worked visually and also figuratively, because the sun's gravity is twenty-eight times our own at its surface, and the goal here was to use gravity to my advantage, the way NASA sends a robotic spacecraft to a nearby planet for a gravity assist to boost the trajectory. The sun's gravitational pull on Earth is only 0.0006 times the strength of gravity on the Earth's surface—but it's good enough to drag our planet into orbit around itself. I conjured thoughts and gravity yanked them in. *Whoosh,* went the lady. Sometimes a "picture-image" bounced back, but no problem, I threw it in again. It was a little cultic, but I liked the lady's company. There was all this fun new terminology, and because I'd chosen to suspend my disbelief—and wanted to get my money's worth—I let myself be absorbed into their sun philosophy and I threw my memories out. It was like putting household items on the street and watching them quickly disappear.

It would be worth it if I could become more cheerful without medication. The guide said she used to have an argument with the world. She was angry at all corners of her soul: "I'm happier," she said calmly. "You have an open mind. You'll do well here." This made me panic midsession and return to Earth. My feet reappeared, and my hands, which I'd watched burn away, per her instructions, grew back as if I were regenerating my starfish limbs. My beanbag chair reappeared, along with my then-teenager, Jerry, dog, house, work, and housework.

As the guide explained it: We see each event in our past through picture-images, but they are only one perspective of the event. It's like Plato's shadows in the cave, said another. This approach seemed logical, intellectual, and because it was an emotional analog to Cubism, it promised to be theoretically radical. Every moment is a photograph, and you need more than one photograph of an occasion or a memory to see it fully—but we tend to hang onto a moment and build a mythology around it. How happy I was that day at the beach, or: How dare he push me!

You don't see the pained memories clearly in those picture-images; you only see who you were in that situation. Maybe that day at Juhu Beach was so profoundly lovely because you got a bumpy ride on an exciting, filthy camel and then had kulfi. Maybe your boyfriend pushed you because you had sex with his New York City friend after your boyfriend had sex with his LA friend, and he only pushed you after you pushed him so hard that he fell onto the sharp tools in his garage and the reason all of this happened was because you were both angry that the relationship was over and you were looking for comfort. It is so easy to hold onto a single story about an event and cement it into your memory as a photograph or as photographic memory.

In *Hold Still: A Memoir with Photographs*, photographer Sally Mann talks about the treachery of photography in the role of memory. "Photography would seem to preserve our past and make it invulnerable to the distortions of repeated memorial superimpositions, but I think that is a fallacy: photographs supplant and corrupt the past, all the while creating their own memories." Mann recognized that it was more interesting to fictionalize reality than to merely capture a moment of reality. It wasn't what was happening anyway. She knew that every photograph was a curation of time and reality, so it was, in its way, already a fiction. She conveyed what she saw with the intrigue and aesthetics of wet-plate collodion, a nineteenth-century process that uses large glass plates and a view camera. "When shooting with collodion, I wasn't just snapping a picture. I was fashioning, with fetishistic ceremony, an object whose ragged black edges gave it the appearance of having been torn from time itself."

It is so often the illusion with art that you think you have captured something that was there all along. But art and memory don't really work that way. Nothing ever ends up exactly how you approached it first, in your mind or on the page. Luck, says Mann,

> is just the ability to exploit accidents. I grew to welcome the ripply flaws caused by a breeze or the tiny mote of dust, which ideally would settle right where I needed a comet-like streak, or the emulsion that peeled away from the plate in the corner where I hadn't liked that telephone line anyway. Unlike the narrator in *Swann's Way* praying for the angel of certainty to visit him in his bedroom, I found myself praying for the angel of uncertainty. And many times she visited my plates, bestowing upon them essential peculiarities, persuasive consequence, intrigue, drama, and allegory.

I began to consider that my memories were not in fact my story—they was only ever a constructed story. I was the one who added the intrigue. I was the one who worried about the drama. The exercise of throwing things out gnawed at me, because it seemed more efficient to add perspective to the memory instead of just tossing it (only to return). I liked the idea of complicating memory the way Mann complicated the stories in her photographs. The nature of memory is Ovidian anyway—it transforms over time as we fill in more of the story. To throw a memory out is to abbreviate experience and preclude the sublime and uncomfortable truths that arrive so slowly.

Their methodology did one thing well: it asked my brain to move faster than my brain—synapses fired, my brain called up a memory, my brain threw out the memory, my brain called up another memory, my brain threw out another memory. Maybe the process would become rote and I'd kick out thoughts as soon as they arrived, but I don't think I'll ever beat my brain at what it does so effectively.

It seems like a great fix to chuck out memories of bullies on the playground and the lovers who broke our hearts, but not many of us want to remember those times when we were cruel, and when we were too emotionally impoverished to care for others when they needed us. How dare we throw our cruelties away instead of living with them! Neither would we want to throw away the tender moments we share with our children, the way they say, "I love you," when we tuck them in. The amorphous beanbag chair oozing around my house had value to my son, Jerry was valuable to me even when we argued, the house was imperfect but it was mine, and the housework needed to be done. I wouldn't want to toss out the sound of my grandmother chanting, the feeling of lift as a plane leaves a runway, the view of the Rockies from the Maroon Bells, the taste of fresh apple juice in the Himalayas, the eyelet ankle-length graduation dress that made me feel so pretty, my son's distracted gaze while he waited for me to take a photograph so he could resume his hunt for frogs and snakes, or the way soft, diffused light hit his young cheekbones at the Audubon Society in Cape Cod on that day he held a box of baby turtles with gleeful and nervous awe, unaware that his dad had just left me. How complicated are our memories.

I'd committed to this program, so I went through the process seriously. I learned that if I threw away my picture-images repeatedly, I'd achieve some distance from them. I could go faster than my brain! (Repetition dulled my brain a little.) Whatever argument I'd had with Jerry played like a movie reel in the distance in proportion to the times I threw it away. I lost interest in the argument. It was easy enough to transform that "picture" of our argument into something more benign, even lovely. How handsome he is when he concentrates, how passionately he talks about William Faulkner, how kind he is when I am angry. Maybe it's true that if I discard every memory and every attachment, I will cruise along on happier feelings, but it is also possible that I will end up with no feelings at all.

It is a coincidence that I ended up at this meditation center because one of my coping skills is throwing things away. During a traumatic time in my life, a therapist suggested that I write down the hateful garbage-y feelings on a piece of paper, rip it to shreds, and bury it deep in the garbage before bed. For months, my hand moved violently across the page, drawing giant jagged letters that formed rants full of swears, or death mail to people who had hurt me. I squeezed every tormented feeling out and it worked. Eventually, I realized that I could just solve problems over email before they got to me at night. I quit jobs, canceled plans, and ended transactional relationships in five minutes, whooshing away the stress with decisive, accusing sentences. So it was curious that I ended up at a place with a strategy of throwing things away, because I was so good at it already. The link between their philosophy and mine was self-preservation.

In addition to the one-hour sales pitch for the meditation philosophy, and the two-hundred-dollar down payment for a month of "meditation," I attended three two-and-a-half-hour private sessions with two women with mid-vocal-range voices and gentle faces. It would take approximately fifty sessions before throwing away becomes second nature, said one, and if you come every few days, every week, for one year, you'll achieve all the stages and then you will be happier. *Whoosh.* Their philosophy was rooted in an idea that you pass through seven levels of "discarding" to escape the illusionary world you were living in, and to eliminate the self (you) who is living in that world. Finally, you become part of the universe. It felt reliably Eastern in that being dutiful and working hard to achieve righteousness would help you reach nirvana.

I was definitely happier after the first week. I avoided the semi-guided "classes" in a dark room where strangers sat on legless BackJack floor chairs and threw their memories into the magnetic sun together. I preferred the social interaction with the women, and hoped we would be friends and that they would invite me to the potluck parties and "hang-out zones."

They told me to go ahead and try other types of "meditation." Other approaches wouldn't work because breathing exercises were temporary, and throwing away picture-images was permanent. I wondered if this was a ruse (if you love something, let it go), but I liked the idea that if I committed to this philosophy, I'd react to irritating situations or relationships with a shrug. I could simplify caring.

Doubt kicked in and I got sick over the weekend. (I never get sick.) One of the meditation ladies texted me to feel better and said if I do the meditation I will get sick less often. I knew they were quietly panicking because the end of the month was nearing and they hoped to lock me into the monthly two-hundred-dollar commitment. She said she believed that I was so open-minded because I was Indian. But I was the opposite: skeptical, fact-based, and closed-minded about Eastern-facing Western philosophies that seem like mail order pets; just add water.

I wanted to breathe. *In*, two, three, four; *out*, two, three, four. I liked oxygen, photosynthesis, the real-life company of my father and son, Jerry's embraces, the sound of my keys turning in the lock of my house. I liked my green Adirondack chair and my biased unreal photographic memory of that week in an Indian hill station named Ooty where my parents bought me a striped walking stick with a carved lion head that I used in the woods to pretend I was a mountain climber. I loved that white eyelet dress. I stopped going to the sessions. The woman who did the sales pitch said no problem; they were there if I changed my mind. I felt bad I wouldn't see her again. The other woman kept calling. She asked me to come in to talk about my decision.

My dad's British-born wife, a self-proclaimed meditation expert and hands-on healer who had studied for years at ashrams in India, told me that the problem with this meditation philosophy was the fact that they were telling me to fill my mind with clutter in order to discard it. Meditation is supposed to empty the mind. Clutter is not supposed to be a prelude to meditation. She once told me that she could meditate herself into Theta, a deep relaxation state in which brain waves slow to four to eight cycles per second. (We all exist in Beta State, from fourteen to thirty cycles per second.) My brain probably moves at the upper end of Beta. Theta is used in hypnosis and associated with REM sleep. Her pitch made sense to me. I had to learn to meditate. I blocked the meditation lady's number.

The following week, I went to my father's house to visit his wife. She would teach me to really meditate. We sat down for ten minutes to breathe, and I slumped a little but breathing felt natural, as if she were a ventriloquist for my body. My mind emptied immediately. Five minutes later I was tired, as she had predicted, and I lay down on the rose-colored carpet. I awoke a half hour later, flattened. I'd fallen into the deepest, dreamless, most motionless sleep I'd had in years. Heavy as a rock, empty headed, I crawled into the living room and said, my god, what have you done?

We all want catharsis, rescue, company, safety, calm, happiness, certitude, faith. No cult or commune will ever be enough, but the compassion of a stranger in an empty room helps a little. But even this is not available unless you have two hundred dollars. *Whoosh* goes the membership. *Whoosh* go the friends and the potlucks and the quiet room.

Part III

Becoming Relentless

The Ability to Oppose

It was a cold Thursday in February, the first clear night of the week that we were spending in Texas Hill Country. We were twelve miles west of Main Street in Llano, where the cadence of life shifts according to the volume of water the river carries. Llano was established in 1856 under a live oak by a bridge, and developed, in its boom years after mineral deposits were discovered on Iron Mountain, into a frontier trading center and steel town, and later into the hamlet it is now. Our rented house was two miles from the road. Rattlesnakes and coral snakes slunk in the scrub around the house, armadillos hid in the leaves, and white-tailed deer watched for coyotes lurking in the dusty ranch across the lane, in fields humming with cattle that wandered out now and then through breaks in the fence. Cattle grazed below old blue skies and knew seasons by the winds that rattled the branches of harboring ash, oak, and sumac trees.

Jerry, a native Texan, slung two wool blankets over his shoulder and strode ahead. My son followed close in his footsteps to avoid spiders and snakes. Jerry always seems to know when poisonous snakes are near, and steps carefully, flashlight first, around outcroppings of roots, patches of scrub, or swampy ground. For him, danger arrives early because he has thought about it for a long time already. As I made my way to the river to join them, I was pleased to use the slim flashlight I'd packed for occasions like tonight. I didn't mind that they'd gone ahead, because the night sky is something you see, and remember, alone. Maybe I hung back on purpose, as if anticipating a celestial sign of love.

I was wearing clogs and the ground was uneven. Big, deranged stars hung seemingly within grasp. Briefly I was startled: looking up into a galaxy from which light pulsed from thousands of years earlier, I felt the brevity of my short life and its aftermath. Time was bending. I've always felt when I'm close to the sky that the end of days is waiting for me. There is a risk of disappearing in the deepest parts of nature, even when the landscape is pretty.

The spring-fed river was low, contracted by cool temperatures. The owner had built a wooden platform by the water, with a bench on two sides. I reclined on the bench, wrapped in a blanket, and stared at the sky. The sky did not seem to be in front of me. Stars bulged and receded all at once. They were in orbit while I was in orbit, and suddenly I could feel it: my body was a sheet of glass while my cognitive awareness remained three-dimensional, and even that was naive. The human eye can see three miles up from a flat surface. If I were a satellite or a meteor with telescopic eyes instead of these sacs of protein and water, I could see more light and resolve the picture.

The mechanics of the universe were illuminated and jitterbugging. I knew I wouldn't be out there long, because it was cold, and my job was to memorize the sky, to scan it like a machine. This is one way to build a planetarium, by stitching together the parts that are too many and that you alone can't recreate or in one glance perceive. No way of seeing will ever be sufficient. We may never be able to resolve the picture. Our minds are blunt tools, but some of the systems we're given possess a certain grace—the eye has a wider field of vision than a telescope, but it cannot sharpen its focus the way a telescope can. I despise my craven searches for joy that resemble all searches for joy, but I love them too; if I could design my outlook with bigger apertures to let the light in and sharpen my view, the emotions of the day might roll along more easily—but then I would not be using the wisdom of the bones and organs my mother grew.

The night sky was strobing with stars, but it didn't resemble the sky back East, at my home in New York City. I was no longer sure how to distinguish what was true from what was scientific. Both states are in the Northern Hemisphere, yet this was not my hemisphere. It had a structure of dissonance and complexity as if it were a harp whose strings had discovered that they could rearrange their molecules and so they continually repositioned themselves around the music they were playing as they played it—I mean, we are all in orbit, and even time itself is not in control.

My son would soon be old enough to get a driver's license, marry, leave. Nothing would be the same from now on. I'd been fired the week before I left New York, right after being diagnosed with a degenerative disease that could kill me. There is no one truth about the job—we are all correct and incorrect in our own ways—but if you are a writer, you have to claw and fight over what you believe in or life loses its electricity. Nietzsche observed that we are quick to sum up others as beneficial or injurious, as good or evil, "but upon a great reckoning, when we consider the whole, we become suspicious of this neat division, and in the end abandon it." My reckoning feels so constant that I am always abandoning and reorganizing my feelings and the beliefs that emerge from my attachment to those feelings. I feel conflict knowing that there are stars above me when some of them are dead already.

The truth is that I took a job at a magazine that seemed to care about books in the same ways that I cared about them, but they were in the business of promoting books, not the contradictory and torn-apart truths inside the books. I had a shaggy attitude and a precision-bomber way of fixing problems. I took the job because I ached for security, which doesn't exist, though we all long for it in our square rooms inside polygonal homes with chameleon loves that never fill us up, inside green-box lawns planted on subdivided, mortgaged, and refinanced histories. I wanted to neutralize my suffering with a nine-to-five job. I wanted to have a conversation with books, and to feel included. I didn't like seeing quick and loose takes on books that authors like me spent years trying to get right, and I didn't value what the company valued. I was there for six months, an eternity.

It is also true that I was beginning to realize that my mind would forever pursue love and conflict equally. In *The Joyous Science*, Nietzsche says, the "ability to oppose, to not have a bad conscience about being hostile toward the familiar, the traditional and the sacrosanct," is "the most important step for the liberated spirit." Besides the fact that Nietzsche had a miserable life, by this standard I was no longer fit for much of anything besides writing if I wanted to have a heightened intellectual life. I wanted to argue with sunshine and clouds and everyone around me. I wanted to argue as a way of being attentive and caring about things. Being oppositional means that when you are demonized in a company evaluation with typos in it, if you're clean in your conscience and if you are an examining person, you do not take it in stride.

Llano gave me peace in the wake of these overlapping tragedies. The trip was a paean to Texas itself, and my way of promising to visit Jerry's world more often rather than living in mine all the time. We hadn't been getting along for months. We had started reading *Paradise Lost* together in December—we were both drawn to books about the experience of sin and the loss of innocence and the ways in which they do not always overlap. I suspect that we were trying to deepen the dialogue we were both having with our writing, a conversation that pitched the inner life against the pathologies of the societies we inhabit and which try to convince us that life works out swimmingly if you adhere to traditional ways of doing things. Jerry was interested in exploring the incantatory monologues of preachers in the South. I was curious about preaching to the reader as a way of solving an argument with myself. My son was growing into an acutely observant person who would not be influenced. He had a natural talent for analytical reasoning, and took logical and measured approaches to problem-solving. He wanted to be a physicist.

For my entire career, I'd put off reading *Paradise Lost*, and would have preferred to put it off a little longer. I worried that it would confound me: I'd mess up the strands of thought, get mired in the complexity that Milton brought with his expansive, musically gifted mind. I'd lose my way, I'd be bored, I'd find myself distracted every five minutes while others simply found their way, and my failure would represent the many ways in which people are proven not up to their task.

Fate throws caveats and surprises at you. The weeks that overlapped with the beginning of our reading *Paradise Lost* were all limbo, marked by my new diagnosis: I had lupus. The bloodwork gave a numerical form to my mortality: my organs no longer had the same capacity to ward off attacks. Before leaving for Texas, I was measured for compression socks—my rheumatologist told me to wear them on the plane to guard against blood clots. "If you are short of breath," she said firmly, holding my gaze to express her seriousness, "go straight to the emergency room from the airport."

Reading *Paradise Lost* would give me exactly what I needed: a grander story than the one I was living. It reminded me that verse was the vessel for my rhythm and beat, and reading the epic poem was my way of paying homage to the thing that had for so long invigorated my being: the line. Milton made jazz of the line and made the vernacular epic. Milton enjambs and unfolds (uncoils) his lines, and with them his syntax—like no poets before him and few poets since. This aligned with what I was good at: writing iambs, spondees, and transitive verbs that trick you out of the traditional singsong and, by opposing, end it. When Milton leaps off into the white space of the air, that is where he, like Satan, like all of us, is falling.

With the first and the final books of his epic, Milton brackets his belief in propulsive individualism. He starts with Satan and ends with Adam and Eve. In book I, Satan falls through an abyss for nine days before arriving in Hell. His rebellion did not mark a loss of faith in God and Heaven but a loss of innocence. He believed that Heaven was a meritocracy, just as I have always believed that good work should be rewarded in a society that functions, at least on the surface, as a meritocracy. It is critical to Milton's vision that Satan has not lost faith in himself. He pronounces, upon arrival:

> The mind is its own place, and in itself
> Can make a Heav'n of Hell, a Hell of Heav'n.

In Book XII, before God's messenger, the archangel Michael, leads Adam and Eve out of Paradise, Michael relates to Adam "the sum of wisdom"—knowledge of all the tyrannies and carnage to come. This is a trick. Knowledge is not so terrific; not at all. Michael advises Adam: if you add to your knowledge deeds, faith, virtue, patience, temperance, love, and charity, you shall "possess a paradise within thee, happier far." It is your actions that are meaningful. It is how you discharge your free will and how you are disobedient, and for what right cause, that changes everything under the stars. The real paradise, beyond Earth and Eden, depends on your heart. Like Satan dusting himself off and rallying his troops in the sulfurous muck, full of passion but not yet a demon, like Adam and Eve stepping forward into a savage landscape on "their solitary way," I too will make my way into my future, happier far.

I am in Llano, Texas, at 10 p.m. on a Thursday in February. This situates me in all four dimensions. I see my son grow into the age I am now and imagine him remembering me then. I see my sister's face ghosting toward me the morning we buried our mother, and our terrace in Bombay where we twirled sparklers on Diwali. I see my father, age fifteen on the night when India become independent and colonialism ended. I see my mother sketching the contours of branches and women's backs. The nudes always faced away from the viewer or they crouched over on the edge of a bed or chair, and it seemed to me that she was sketching herself. My son is looking into a telescope at an observatory where he works, at the same stars we saw in Llano but with a greater depth of field and a parallax view of galaxies that have grown familiar to him. Sometimes he lies outside in a dark-sky reserve, to see the stars with his own eyes. Earth has grown hotter. Parts of the world have dipped underwater to become lost cities. Wildfires consume hectares. Dust storms, God's whirlwind, have ravaged the American Midwest. Much of the world has migrated north. My son remembers a night when the air was cold and the river was low and I was still alive, looking forty trillion kilometers up, with him, into our galactic frontier. I've lost my depth perception now; depth no longer makes sense even as a word; really, it is just death; and there is no longer a house on stilts or a riverbank or even the two men in my life, nearby in the dark.

Perhaps my self-pity was encouraging me to mourn my overlapping tragedies in Texas. But things don't always unfold in the way you imagine. Instead I found more possibilities. I smelled mesquite, dirt, and sweet river air. Stars drizzled around me; when I reached out to catch them, they snapped back to the horizon. From the platform by the river on a clear February night, we might have seen Sirius, the Dog Star, 8.6 light years away. It struck me that the light from some of the stars and star systems had taken my entire life to arrive. During the then-sixteen years of raising my son, I'd never once told him Earth was spinning. What I understand, now, is that life takes a long time, for the stars and for me. Who you're predestined to become is no short journey.

Milton's narrative is a story of disappearances—not about the place you leave but the place you occupy next. I have a spot on Earth but am in constant orbit, so my perspective is forever changing. If disobedience is Milton's definition of evil, I have no quarrel with that evil. I know I'm not a demon, because Satan taught me to recognize the kingdom in myself. I fell so hard in love with him. He is the hero for longing to be loved and treated well. I knew the story beforehand, but didn't expect Satan to be so heroic or Eve to take so much initiative. Being disobedient for the right reasons will not mitigate your suffering. What matters is how you react to circumstances in the process of becoming. "You shall become who you are," Nietzsche says.

It was a peculiar provocation to feel that at my mightiest moment of recognizing my complete lack of power, time was arcing and bending around me. There was no way to understand what was happening in the sky. Some stars revealed themselves for the last time, and others for the first. The oldest stars I could see with my eyes appeared just as they had four thousand years earlier. That knowledge was critical to the register of the night. I was in fellowship with something unusual.

The disease I was traveling with had already been with me for months or, quietly, for years, and the only difference between the time before the blood test and now was information. It was time to heal and embrace my personality as a relentless person in pursuit of experience. "Indulge your best and worst desires and above all perish!" Nietzsche suggests. I told myself that I would live with this new terminology—lupus is a condition of rebellion in the body, but as Satan said, the mind can make a heaven out of hell. I would embrace my newfound freedom to set aside the kinds of work I didn't enjoy and puzzle out the process of loving more diligently. I would recognize that I was an opposing person who took love in like a sieve and held nothing in my shaky orbit. How will anyone love a woman like that? I'm not dead yet, but I'm happier still.

I trekked up the path, indifferent to the boggy grass and loose rocks, and didn't look up again. I walked between the stilts that kept the house standing when the river rose, and banged my clogs hard on the stairs going up.

Conversations about Art

I dozed on a single bed at my aunt's apartment in Bombay and listened to the soft violence of the rains through flung-open windows. Storm clouds devoured the light and cast my room a purple-gray, and I did not know if I'd awake to boiling fortissimo rains or the fizzling shreds of a rainbow. Monsoon skies are unpredictable. My aunt sat at the dining table outside my room, revising an article on Jain frescoes on deadline. Her presence consoled me. This aunt was a scholar of Jain art—she'd written a dozen books and hundreds of articles on the subject, founded the National Gallery of Modern Art in Bombay, and championed young artists. I'd met her once, decades earlier, when her husband—my father's first cousin—was alive.

I was eager but nervous to stay with this aunt because on the surface she seemed intimidating and stern. I'd planned a two-week trip for research I was conducting about life in the forties, and was hoping to sponge up something undefinable that I couldn't find in books. As a favor to my father, this aunt offered to house me, and took pains to help me with my research by setting up appointments, joining me on drives to neighborhoods that had not been transformed since the forties, and accompanying me to galleries to get a feel for the art scene so I could project it onto a character in my novel. I also wanted to buy a painting.

When I first arrived, I didn't know that I was a gift: my father's gift to share me with her, and her gift to care for me unconditionally for him. They had not shared that quality of caring in fifty years. Their relationship had diminished because of my mother, whose impatience changed the dynamics of my father's relationships in Bombay. My mother had been dead for seventeen years when I flew to Bombay to stay with this aunt. In the novel I was researching, the married couple that resembled my parents would suffer a break, and after much turmoil and adventure, they would slowly and with plenty of uncertainty rediscover one another. My real parents stayed together for forty years—seven of which they lived in India—but they never discovered enough varieties of one another to thrive as a couple.

When I woke up, I smelled cotton, anise, ghee, and mustard. It was sunny out but the humidity was building. I rolled to my side, flexed the muscles in my thighs, swung my feet to the floor, felt for my slippers, and stood up. The cook would be making chapatis for me. Geetha, who ran the household, would appear with a broad smile and a bowl of papaya and pomegranates. She'd pinch my cheek as if I were a child, though I had a teenager myself. My aunt would ask how my nap was.

I straightened my back to avoid getting scolded for bad posture, and drew the first set of muslin curtains behind the glass doors of the guest room, drew the second set of heavier wheat-gold curtains, and jiggled the door gently, as instructed. It slid apart without harming the wood frame that had thickened in the humidity, and I stepped out.

The machinery of the household kicked in. It struck me that a lot of arrangements had been made on my behalf. Three thousand miles away, my father was keeping track of my weeks there, in a mutually agreed upon tacit understanding with my aunt. An older woman hadn't cared for me properly for a long time, not since we lived in Bombay. My mother had never emerged from the quicksand of depression that took hold of her there.

My aunt showed me the manuscript she was working on with childlike enthusiasm, explaining that the fresco was unusual because it depicted a woman reaching nirvana—nothing like it existed. Her eyes shone over these ancient hand-drawn frescoes made from vegetable pigments. (In Jainism, women must be reborn into men before they can reach nirvana. No Jain has reached nirvana in more than 2,500 years.) My aunt was in her eighties, and as she toiled over her proofs, she grumbled that writing took her so long—she was getting older, she should give it up—but then she promptly took on another assignment. Every morning we worked together at the table.

Her flat was spare, with bare walls and a living room cut with a series of double doors to a balcony that right-angled around the building. My aunt was thinking of hanging new art by young and emerging artists to replace the paintings by artists she'd discovered or collected over her career, and which she had removed from the walls. Perhaps she wanted to feel what the younger artists were feeling. You don't choose young artists unless you want to soak up the adrenaline of their raw, limber, and energetic minds. Young artists do not have the authority of older artists—and they certainly don't have the transcendence—but authority gets boring. The unpracticed conversations that uncelebrated artists are having with their work is a reminder that inexperience is promising. Perhaps this is doubly important when you are hunched over your work with the windows open and the humidity fills the rooms instead of your husband of fifty years.

I'd set aside five hundred dollars to buy a painting, following the example of my mother sixty years earlier. She'd earned a small salary from teaching part-time at the Bombay International School and then as an English teacher at the German school. My father told her that they didn't need her salary for household expenses, so she spent it on art. "She had a good eye and she bought what she liked," he said. Gallerists told her about upcoming artists, and except for one M. F. Husain painting that my father bought for 750 rupees (approximately $80 in 1967 and $10 now), my mother bought all of her paintings with her own money. It must have felt bittersweet to know that as a foreigner and expat with limited independence, she was able to purchase work by artists she cared about even while not getting serious about her own creative work. My father bought her the painting by Husain because he thought my mother resembled the woman in the painting. (Husain, the celebrated and controversial Indian Muslim painter whose work sold for millions, went into self-exile because of the virulent response to his irreverent depictions of Hindu deities.)

It was an expression of tenderness for my father to give my mother a painting whose subject resembled her, even if he didn't share her interests. It was a concrete way to connect. Our family was not without love, but love was not in our family vocabulary, and expressions of love came in other ways: German candy, sparkly bangles, ten paisas for a paper cone filled with peanuts, temperature-taking on days we were sick, trips to Juhu Beach and money for camel or elephant rides. My parents had fallen in love, but to my eyes, their relationship had aspects of the arranged marriages that foregrounded the Indian family unit. Yet there was a difference between Indian mothers and my mother. Indian mothers cared for their children with proximity and affection. My mother cared for me with proximity and without affection. Instead, she cultivated my critical sensibility—without an opinion and a critical eye, she taught me, you were nothing; you had no grounding, no broad strokes, no intellectual view. What if I, while in Bombay, could find something valuable, just like she did? I would find an affordable painting with promise and a point of view.

Several weeks passed at the dining table. One morning, my aunt gazed at me and said I looked exactly like my mother. It was a complicated moment because she also confessed that that my father had stopped spending time with her after returning from New York with his new bride in tow. "Your mother never wanted much to do with me," she said, and waited for my reaction. She tried to interest my mother in social events—she was becoming well known in certain circles back then, my aunt said with pride, and a lot of interesting people were eager for her company—but my mother had no interest in the friendship.

Her revelation pained me because I was a gift between two households, and because she had concealed her feelings for more than forty years. I was in Bombay to recover something for myself, but it turns out I was also there for my father and for her. She said, generously: "Your father and I saw each other less frequently after that." My father told me later that in the seven years we lived in Bombay, she came for dinner twice.

There was nothing to do but apologize on behalf of my mother and then on behalf of my father. "I have just discovered you," I said, either in my voice or in my heart. But I secretly emailed my father while my aunt and I spoke, and asked why my mother hadn't wanted to spend time with her. If she'd had more intellectual company, maybe she'd have been happier. She'd have emerged from the air-conditioned room she continually vanished into, and kept that toothless boogeyman who wore a lungi and lived on a plank above the stairwell of the apartments in the converted garage behind our building from chasing me. She'd have told the servants of the landlord to lay off the games where they tried to touch me in the private rooms. She'd have held my hand and let me sleep in her bed until I was twelve, and if she had kept drawing, her subject would have been me.

Many of the aunts in my immediate family were less educated or less artistic than this aunt, who was from a different wing of the family. During family gatherings when I was young, the women didn't have much to talk about besides their children and their ailments. It was obvious that my mother was bored. But I loved the easy silence of drinking tea and eating digestives or chakri while the men sat cross-legged on the floor playing Bukharo.

It bothered me that my mother wasn't friendlier to this aunt. She was not an intellectual back then, my father said in an email. She most definitely is an intellectual, I countered with loud clacks at 103 words per minute. My irritation at my dead mother rose. Here was one more thing that my mother tore apart and which I had to patch together somehow. But my father has a remarkable memory. "She was a dutiful wife to an extremely wealthy man," he wrote, and said she'd became known in her field only after he and my mother left India. I reread his reply now, looking for a way out, another answer. The truth is that she had an art degree back then but probably was not yet established. He was voicing what my mother understood intuitively, and standing by my mother because he had admired her intellect, even if he had not always admired the way she presented herself: electric, snappy, contemptuous, precise. She did not care about small talk and she did not like very many people. My aunt remembers that my mother did not care for her, and she was correct.

I argued with my father over email every morning, trying to change our family story. "We sit here with our breakfast and talk about Jainism, writing, and history," I wrote. "She has contacted a curator to help me with my research on art deco buildings and has brought me to all the top galleries with her art historian friends. She has good taste," I clacked, "just as good as mom's. She knows those same artists whose paintings mom bought in the sixties and which now fill my house." (Just as my aunt has gotten rid of her paintings, so has my father.) "She knows which artists will become stars and which ones will dry up. She answers my questions with a certitude that implies a munificence of spirit."

She has lived an interesting life by any count, I thought. In a generation when women were frowned on for being ambitious, you had to be brave to do as you pleased. "She left India to study art history in the States. She started a museum, edited a magazine, and built her life around art. She has curated and consulted for museums in many countries." *She still publishes while you are in retirement*, I thought. "Right now she is writing the only article ever published about the only Jain fresco ever done that reveals a woman attaining nirvana."

I thought this list of achievements would help. My father has a palatial memory and what appears to be bionic vision in hindsight, and he sees the world taxonomically. Before I left New York, he showed me his list of medical procedures: 50 CAT scans, 135 blood tests, 18 MRIs. He adjusted to old age and tracked it like the clinician he is. I'd hoped that I could impress upon him her success and maybe mend the rift in their relationship a little. But it wasn't clear that he saw it as a rift—and she had said enough. Hovering between the emails that my father and I exchanged was my absent brilliant mother, twice the intellect of most people around her and carefree about it, like a hawk who could see what you could not. Poised to kill, she could scissor the air at top speed, but she was klutzy about sustaining the love she so clearly needed at close range.

❧ ❧

When I told my aunt that I wanted to shop for a painting, she drilled me on the styles, artists, shapes, and colors I liked—in the same way my mother might have—before taking me on the rounds in South Bombay's maze-like and trendy art district known as Kala Ghoda.

Gallerists of all ages dropped what they were doing and raced over to greet my aunt when she walked in, chatting her up and inviting her to openings. (She seemed to attend all of them, and despite her bad knees she was always on the move.) At one white-cube gallery, I pointed at a floor-to-ceiling painting and asked how much. "You have good taste," my aunt said with a smile. We went to a dozen galleries where everything was beyond my budget—though my aunt tried to convince me that a twenty-thousand-dollar painting would be a good investment for an up-and-coming artist who she believed in. "Five hundred dollars," I said. I went home empty-handed.

The function of art is impossible to define: to confront, dissect, rupture, experiment, juxtapose, interpret, reimagine, and express. It requires you to have a conversation with the tools you are using to negotiate the resources at your disposal, whether those resources are words, paint, sound, material, or film. You do what is familiar and fall in love with your ideas for a while, and then, as you evolve, you attack your stale ideas and do something unfamiliar. If you are greedy, and you should be greedy, you keep siphoning gas from your experience and use it.

When you are young, your ears, eyes, skin, and feet take the world in all at once, and you believe that something out there is waiting for you. Back to my aunt's feeling of wanting paintings by young artists on the wall and my mother's pleasure over buying paintings by young artists with the money she earned. We record our lives on the grid of a canvas, the space of a ledger, the pages of a novel. Do those artifacts hold more truth about experience than experience itself? There are no boundaries to thinking. You never get to the end of color, line, and space. You hope for that from people, but people have limitations.

❧ ❧

I went to India to discover the world of the 1940s, but the real reason was to recapture the childhood that inspired the book I was writing about my parents. I wanted to fictionalize and reimagine my childhood, and everything else was incidental.

The conversation with my dad continued over email every morning and I got more of the story. Back then, he explained, this aunt was not yet the sort of person that mom found common ground with intellectually. My aunt also spoke too much Gujarati among friends, which excluded my mother. Shunning her might have been a way for my mother to retaliate. If she'd given my aunt a chance, maybe their mutual passion for art would have cheered my mother or inspired her to continue drawing.

My mother's drawings of fleshy, vulnerable women and naked trees seemed larger than the measure of the paper. She loved expressionist painters: Max Beckmann, Oskar Kokoschka, and Egon Schiele—truth-tellers of a world askew. I, too, appreciated their provocative subject matter and the ways they moved paint across the canvas: Beckmann's segmented scenes that embody our divided and war-ravaged minds, Kokoschka's figurative shapes that move inside big passages of paint and evoke an amorphous longing, and Schiele's flirtations with porn that reveal a passion for the line and a sexual frankness that is simultaneously piquant and vulnerable. I wanted my mother to care about me as much as she cared about paintings.

Eventually my mother asked to return to America. But after nine years abroad—in Germany and India—she no longer had the credentials to get another teaching job. In New Jersey, she wrote a few articles about art and visited Manhattan galleries and museums with frenzied interest on day trips from our square one-acre two-story house in the stultifying, homogeneous New Jersey suburbs. A decade later, we moved to Connecticut, where she befriended a visual artist and bought two of her cheerfully botanical paintings. My father describes those paintings as "mostly of large leaves." My mother learned to garden, and adjusted to coastal New England life on the shoreline of the Long Island Sound. She wanted something pretty. She cultivated a giant purple-blue hydrangea bush in the yard beside the kitchen window. She bought paintings at yard sales. Perhaps that was enough. Maybe she just gave up. She tossed her charcoals and drawings out. Years later, when she did not have that much time left, my sister and I went to an art store to buy her more charcoals and paper so she'd draw again, but she refused to use them, and eventually she threw them away.

One way to live an artist's life is to make sure you leave something concrete behind, and I'm not saying that objects are more concrete than love. My mother destroyed all the drawings she made, and seemed to want to erase herself before she was erased. If we met now, would she recognize that I was the painting that was valuable, and would she like my point of view?

My aunt approved of the painting I finally bought on my last day: an abstract architectural landscape of a city on a hill, in the foreground, and an ominous foggy section in the back. ("Cubism gets weird," observed an artist friend of the painting.) The painter was a young man named M. Singh. The brushstrokes reminded me of Cézanne's and the blue, black, and white color scheme created variety and emotion with specks of yellow and red. Looking at the paintings my mother bought, I see some resemblances in geometric shapes (squares, circles, and parallelograms) and decisive lines. The difference is that she bought figurative paintings with people who faced her from the frame: a dancing woman, a poet with his pages, a group of people in a court scene. She filled her life with people. For five hundred dollars, I bought a simpler canvas. It was the first piece the artist had sold. It was not valuable, but I liked the abstraction and the colors, and most importantly, it was mine. I was prepared to live with it and keep looking.

Before I left Bombay, I gazed at my aunt, devastated to leave and embarrassed that our family had spent so much of our lives without her. She had clearly adored my father, and now she appeared to adore me, too. I hung the canvas on my wall with the paintings that my parents bought and the trees and the nudes that illustrate themselves so easily in my mind, but which are absent.

Year of the Horse

My earliest memory of Prospect Park is visiting the carousel with my grandmother Rose Lila Macklowe, who used her middle name as her first, and my grandfather Sidney Leonard. She wore plum-red lipstick and a beehive hairdo, and I associated her with Campbell's chicken soup, smiling, and Abraham Lincoln, which was the name of their building at 61 Eastern Parkway in Brooklyn. Across the street, from left to right, were all the monumental institutions that turned rural Brooklyn into a desirable city: the Brooklyn Botanical Gardens, the Brooklyn Museum, and the Brooklyn Library, which occupies the northeast corner of Prospect Park, which begins at Grand Army Plaza.

My grandmother smeared her lipstick on thick, and she smiled so much that I wondered if she did this to show off the color of her lips. There was always an outing when my sister and I visited, and the best was when our grandparents took us to ride the carousel, a riot of sound and color inside a partially enclosed brick building in the park. We hung onto the railings outside, watching the carousel revolve, and the moment the ride was over and everyone cleared out, all the children, including me, ran to find the horse they wanted. The carousel had fifty-three ornate hand-carved wooden horses: some were stationary, others moved up and down gently on poles, and a handful really charged. I wanted to ride the largest horse and to experience the adrenaline of moving fast. I'd slip my feet into the stirrups, look around for my sister, and wait for the wild horses to buck and gallop. The Wurlitzer organ started, the platform began to spin, and we were off.

It is the condition of being in Prospect Park that you are always ready for something to happen, and it always does. It is a place where tens of thousands of horses have tread, it is a place of community where Brooklynites came together to renovate the carousel when it fell into disrepair, and it is a place I associate with love.

I have ambled over the same trails or shortcuts a thousand times and still there are surprises. Clouds take new shapes. Commemorative dogwood, magnolia, redbud, and hawthorn trees emerge in spring and fall. Vistas unfold. A tree is halved from lightning, the grass is wet with dew, fences are up again to rejuvenate the fields, bullfrogs growl at cicadas to be quiet, and a cardinal scissors across the shade. If I followed it, I'd run into the transom that cuts across the park from the bridle path and I'd see horses with children on their backs or led by their trainers, as if I did not live in a metropolis. There is only one stable left in Brooklyn now, but in the 1890s, horses hauled passengers to the far reaches of New York City, and they were the economic engine of the nineteenth century. The horses from Kensington Stables, nearby, are huge magnificent beasts with a metronomic clop and long prehistoric spines, and they have always been part of the park's reassuring scenery.

I moved to my neighborhood of Park Slope twenty years ago so that my son could experience messy outdoor days: dirt, mud, grass, turf, rocks, leaves, stumps, twigs, trees, frogs, turtles, ducks, swans, creeks, cataracts, and lakes. In other words, an unruly landscape that wore the seasons on its face and felt them underfoot, and which understood that this was what childhood was about. I wanted to walk through uninterrupted space without the long shadows of one building after another, and I wanted the noise of time to come from the syrinx of swallows, the owls' screech—or *oooo*—and boomboxes that loudly broadcast lyrics from Clipse's "Grindin" ("I'm the neighborhood pusher, call me subwoofer") because life in the park is about community and we share what we do.

My home is one mile from the Abraham Lincoln building, where my grandparents lived. It is specific to living in Brooklyn that you will walk by the histories of a million people every twenty minutes, including your ancestors, and you will learn that the center of Brooklyn is Prospect Park, which itself is a commodity of open space while it offers freedom from material commodities. The park was built to provide fresh air and a healthy environment for people who flocked here in the nineteenth century for jobs in factories—but it was also designed to increase land values and turn the swampland of Brooklyn into a great city.

When my son was young, I took him on the carousel with the galloping horses that I had ridden when my grandparents were alive, and spent long days collecting sticks or sitting in manic playgrounds. He climbed trees and sat there doing nothing like a king. He could spend hours pulling on the branches of elms or maples to shake their helicopter seeds loose, and race to catch them. Aimlessness is part of the plan—of the park's design, of childhood, of leisure. And if you can't forget your worries, the park will distract you; it will loosen your jaw and open your ears to the jazz musicians on one path and the percussionists on another. A trail will lead you one way and you will choose another. After ten years, maybe twenty, you will discover a fountain you have never seen and meet a plein air painter who is duplicating the scene he is standing in. All life passes by on sunny days: extended families grill together, birthday party goers hoist balloons, cyclists and runners pulse along the road that curves behind them. It is easy to take the park for granted, but it is also the job of the park to let you take it for granted.

It doesn't matter if you live in a mansion or a rowhouse, whether you speak English or not, or whether you are alone—you are welcome in Prospect Park because you are on foot and that is what we have in common. Walking in the park is the ultimate leveling, and it has always offered me solace while enlarging my perspective. I had never noticed how wind moved through the park, but one day, I was walking with a friend and a storm churned up, and with it, high wind. He started running, slowing only to yell back that he was afraid of wind. I ran after him. We parted ways and ran home in the rain to keep from melting. During a second walk, when it was windy—but no storm was coming—we paused on a ridge. I wondered if he would bolt. This time, he grinned at me and put his arms out like a hang glider lifting off. I stretched my arms out. A man walking north, fifty meters away, stopped and gazed at us. Suddenly he threw his arms out. The three of us stood there like crosses for five minutes, gliding. He waved goodbye and continued on his way. Being in the park reminds you that if you did not go, you would be lacking for the experience.

There was one time that my ex-husband, Tom, and I brought our child to the park and sat there hopelessly, no different from so many people who were no longer in love, and we helped him collect sticks. I remember that Ivan's father was so peaceful when he threw a baseball to show our son how high and far his dad could throw and I don't know why he didn't just throw fastballs and knuckleballs across the Long Meadow with its rolling vistas all day while the crowd at Fenway Park leaned in and cheered "Home run!"—it was Red Sox versus Yankees, bottom of the ninth, and the pitch was liquid, the ball left Earth and someone retrieved the ball, surprised, and asked Tom if he had thrown it and the ballpark vanished but Tom's eyes shone.

It is the nature of love that we think scenery will take away our pain but it will not. This is why community matters so much. I bought a yellow frisbee with a thick curve at the edges, and set about trying to relearn how to throw a frisbee—I got under it, turning my wrist, contracting my back muscles and dipping my shoulder for a clean toss. Strangers who joined our group eventually brought out giant doughnut saucers that were faster, easier to catch, and did not hit the ground with a clunk—and we filled the hours. Playing catch is a joy because it is something you produce; whether you are an artist or a banker, all you have to do is catch the round ball and remember that life doesn't care if you drop it but it does come around for you. You watch out for frisbees, kickballs, softballs, kites, and volleyballs whizzing by and remember that all the open space was designed not to sequester you but to create interactions.

When the landscape architects Frederick Law Olmsted and Calvert Vaux laid out their visionary plan for 585 acres of recreation space in Brooklyn, in 1866, they wanted to give city dwellers a "sense of enlarged freedom" and relief from "the cramped, confined and controlling circumstances of the streets." Olmsted believed that scenery had an unconsciously restorative effect, says Charles E. Beveridge, the editor of Olmsted's papers. People would feel freer. Segregated social classes would intermingle. Parks would be designed to be democratic spaces that would level difference and encourage social interaction between the classes.

This came true. There is no freedom like the freedom you possess in Prospect Park. No one cares what you wear, the cops keep their distance, people strike up conversations over birds or dogs, and no one bothers you. On weekends, you will see West Indians and South Asians playing cricket, athletes hitting volleyballs, parents chasing children, teenagers smoking weed, track teams training, and toddlers chasing butterflies. There is no country like Brooklyn. There is no outdoor space like a park in the middle of a city built on immigrants.

A communal feeling governs the park because we share the clean air now and we shared the rank air in the nineteenth century. Between 1804 and 1887, there were epidemics every three years: typhoid, cholera, yellow fever. People died here on average at age twenty. Since the infectious disease era in nineteenth-century cities, ventilation has improved and vaccines or other treatments became available, but during the pandemic, the air became rotten again.

Hours-long walks in Prospect Park were a salve during the pandemic. Rich and poor, we came from neighborhoods adjacent to the park for sunlight, moonshine, weather. We avoided other people. We walked with screams on our impassive faces, but eventually we began to notice the landscape around us, and we could almost fast-walk all the hauntings from our systems. Rain made the day unbearably interior, so unless a torrential storm pulled up, it was better to carry an umbrella and get a salvation walk in anyway. The park was rugged, unrefined: mud-stink soured the trails, insects and fungi infested rotted tree trunks, bullfrogs belched. Roughly thirty thousand trees enlivened us and pumped out oxygen. Winter branches struck a chorus line pose, arms up, as if asking us to clap. They exposed their knobby old bodies and threw shadows about.

I appreciate, but do not know how to convey, all the ways in which I was discovering the park and the park was discovering me. Prospect Park vibrated with the tension and love that the empty streets lacked. It listened to what people in their homes wanted to say to one another but couldn't voice. Dread coated the blades of grass, chewed holes in the leaves, and clawed the bark. It bored into the soil and cataracted down untroubled waterfalls to escape the diseased air. The fear of contaminated air that the pandemic generated recalled those dirtiest days of the nineteenth century, when the city had no sewers, Prospect Park didn't exist, and horses roamed the streets and left behind their excrement or, when pushed to the brink, their lifeless carcasses.

In the plan they proposed, Olmsted and Vaux described a system of walks through Prospect Park that would allow pedestrians to "ramble over the whole extent of the property with as much apparent freedom as if the whole park had been intended solely for their enjoyment." For 150 years, the park fulfilled this promise, but rambling in a high-stakes year heightened the need for everyone to figure out what they liked exploring most. I followed my curiosities, too, and became interested in slopes and garden spaces. I could go high for a vista and seek out grand stairways before descending trails I didn't know. I often found myself in the northeastern section of the park, and eventually came across the Vale of Cashmere, a woodland area with three low circular dugouts separated from one another by dogwood trees. It used to be a rose garden with goldfish and lilies in the pools, and before that, it was a children's playground—with the park's very first carousel, driven by a real horse. When the Parks Department let things go, the community stepped in. Similar to the way the nonprofit community group the Prospect Park Alliance had renovated the carousel, the Vale is now in the process of being redesigned and restored by a community group called the Hester Street Grain Collective.

There are so many ways I have missed what was right in front of me. I took for granted the idea that beautiful horses walking by will always be part of the scenery, that the dogwoods will flower free of disease, and that love will keep arriving. I did not look at the woods closely enough, and saw branches and sticks in the thickets as filler—until I noticed that an infrastructure of leisure was under way in every direction. Lean-tos and teepees constructed from felled branches began appearing at an ever-quickening pace. Some shelters were ramshackle and others were so sturdy—with branches trimmed to roughly the same mass and length—that they must have been built by architects. It was against park rules to put up temporary structures, and the park rangers were supposed to tear them down, but I think that people loved them so much that the rangers would have ended up with broken hearts, and so, instead, they contributed. All our homes are temporary. I thought of these structures as giant armadillos, with sheltering armor to protect our bodies against the elements. People exercised outside and teenagers made bike ramps from packed mud and sawed off tree branches in the woods by a chain-link fence—catching air on a mountain bike is so important because when you are fenced in, it is up to you to create a world inside the fence that is larger than the fence and larger than you.

By 2020 Jerry had been living with me for four years. Like most love that begins in Brooklyn, our love began while walking in the park. He lived one neighborhood away. At the time, I'd stopped dating for a year, and had made myself a promise not to have sex with anyone unless I was in love. Either this was a Victorian approach or a paradox, but New York City has always been a place where you can make yourself a ridiculous promise.

(Jerry was a slim marathoner and writer who strode with easy confidence up to our meeting point at the Ninth Street park entrance, wearing a black tee and black jeans just loose enough to reveal his strong pecks and defined gluteus maximus. But all afternoon, instead of kissing me, he kept looking out into Olmsted's wilderness. On our second date we met at a bar, and I noticed that the color of his eyes was repeated in his gray-blue shirt. We went to the park, and again wandered for hours. He was running a half-marathon the next morning, but we made plans for the afternoon, and again met in the park on a warm day designed for exploring, but this time we left immediately because by then it was clear, and the days that followed were a blur, and I knew by Monday that I was in love.)

I usually explored the park alone, but on one weekend in December 2020, Jerry and I set out for a late afternoon walk. I expected more bad news in the world, but I did not expect to amble down a hill, in woods that seemed Edenic compared to the dread that infected everything, and witness a horse in duress. Struggling to her feet behind a blood-red pickup truck, she embodied the relentless suffering that soured the year. Three rangers and one concerned couple gathered near the truck. We stopped on the transverse road to talk to the concerned couple, who had seen the horse fall, and together we waited to see what would happen.

A red sports car drove up and braked abruptly to a halt. A woman in riding boots jumped out in that way that people racing to the site of an accident move because they do not know what to expect, so every second counts more. She moved with emergency energy, but within a few meters of the horse, she slowed her approach. The expert, the friend, the trainer. She stroked the horse's head and the space between its eyes. It nuzzled her and licked her thighs. Her jeans were the color of cornflowers. Also moving quickly was a man with a grizzled brown beard that thinned at the edges. This was Walker, the owner of Kensington Stables.

Walker told the three park rangers, another couple at the scene, and my partner and I that it was not unusual for a horse to fall, but that it was very unusual for a horse to have trouble getting up. He gave her medication to help her to her feet. That was the end of the information. The horse stood there rigid beside the truck, looking as dazed as we felt.

People were returning home from their restorative walks and pandemic exercise, and the sun was setting as usual between heaven and Earth. Branches scribbled the day's eavesdroppings on gray skies. Confused trees attempted to rouse themselves in the unseasonably warm weather.

I was so used to life being on alert that the horse's condition immediately deepened the caved-in feeling that had refused to lift all year. Seeing horses walking by proved that in some unshakable way, the grand design that gives us life and takes it back is about more than who, in a plague, survives. Horses move with shine and rhythm, and they seem like the only sane creatures in the park, because no one who lived through the pandemic in New York feels quite as sane as they used to. Doubling the tragedy was the realization that even in a state of affliction, the horse was expected to walk on trembling legs back to Kensington Stables. She was always alone in a street occupied with cars. She had no idea that Brooklyn used to have thousands of stables and four thoroughbred racecourses in the nineteenth century.

Weeks after I saw the horse on its knees, my oldest friend, Fiona, was diagnosed with terminal cancer of the pancreas and liver. I found out after she started emailing me photographs of myself during college, when I dated her youngest son for two years. In the photograph, I leaned against a tree beside her son, and I looked heavy, dark, rough. "How much a part of my family you were," she wrote, and attached another photograph of her three sons and me at Christmas. I had only one photograph of Fiona, which she gave me one lost day in the thirty-five years we were friends. Young and firm-shouldered, she is grinning in a field, surrounded by horses, and her light pink tank top tucks into a white cotton skirt. The horses' coats look like velour. I took a picture of this picture and sent it to her.

More photos arrived, along with the explanation that she was looking at family photographs because she was dying. "I enjoy everything with more intensity than ever," she wrote, at the end of a year when we held our breath and hoped the air would not infect us, and we hoped that our emaciated lives would eventually grow fuller and less fragile and we would enjoy spending time with other people again.

I continued my walks. A waxing crescent moon appeared that night on the winter solstice. By habit I always looked up to track the moon's varying degrees of illumination in daylight, but during my walk that night, I noticed that the moon appeared to be in an entirely different part of the sky. I was so used to looking at the moon from one direction that I didn't immediately realize that it was I who was moving. You think the moon is within sight all the time, without thinking about the adjustments in the motion you are making in its presence, and then you're surprised when the moon seems to walk off and do its own thing, as if it has deserted you for a while—but it was you, locked in your thoughts, who deserted the moon.

That night the moon was 38 percent illuminated and 397,041.163 kilometers away from everyone who died on Earth. The newspapers did not record the number of dead that day, and instead covered the solstice as if the moon were gone, the night itself were gone—yet the moon would return at its scheduled time on the following day after this shortest and darkest twenty-four hours of the gloomiest year of the century.

The heaviness lifted because Fiona was dying—for a month, I had something urgent to live for. I couldn't feel terrible because she did not feel terrible. She talked about how lucky she was to have lived such a long life, with so much love, and said her ashes will go into the ground in the mountains, on the mesa she loved, and she felt marvelous. New optimism propelled me on my walks because I was looking for something to send her: a photograph of a flower or a pretty corner, a swampy lake with dramatic shadows. I recorded poems and thoughts about our time together and even about her son, who I had not seen since college until we met on Zoom while she was dying. "Thank you for being friends with my mom all these years," he said.

I learned so much from her. Fiona had dated my political science professor for forty-five years on and off, and they had a grand romance and a tender friendship. She taught me how to become a woman and a feminist: I saw from her example that it was not necessary to get married, and you could move in and out of a relationship over time, you could forgive people easily, and you could welcome people into your home and arms and still be alone and happy. You did not need a fortune and you did not need a fabulous house. You needed to know how to get excited about things and you needed to know how to love.

Fiona was born in England in 1932, the daughter of Scottish

parents. When she was nine years old, she and her sister were sent to boarding school in New Brunswick, Canada. Her mother grew up in Jamaica but was sent to England when she was five, and when she was eighteen she married a guy who worked for Shell Oil and who would bring her back to the Caribbean if she married him. They settled in Trinidad. She was the kindest person I have ever known.

❧ ❧

There is always more to know about a person and their intentions. In their 1866 preliminary report to the Brooklyn Board of Commissioners, Olmsted and Vaux outlined a radical circulation system of bridle paths, equestrian roads, and promenades so people could explore the park separately but still glimpse one another. Wide, tree-lined parkways would radiate out from the park and add a beat to the park's greenery space while enticing development around tree-lined parkways. This included Eastern Parkway, where my grandparents lived. It was a democratizing plan. The park would also raise property values and make Brooklyn "the centre of exchanges for the world," they said.

In "The Opportunity of Brooklyn," their plan states plainly that the opportunity was not the park itself. The park would be a restorative, sun-lit place that would attract visitors and filter the air of disease. The opportunity was the development of Brooklyn. Whether it would be occupied by more and wealthier residences depended on the value of the land, they explained, and it was upon that value that Brooklyn's prosperity hinged. In the preliminary report, they press on: it would be easy to miss this opportunity to let the land be given up to "shanties, stables, breweries, distilleries, and swine-yards." Or they could make Brooklyn the most attractive place to live in the metropolis. Attention to the project had already quadrupled the land value, they said.

Now that Brooklyn, population 2.7 million, is a center of exchanges for the world, I wonder if the promise of Olmsted and Vaux's vision—sinewy paths through forested ravines, small cataracts shivering into ponds, unfolding views—was so effective because it was artificial. Olmsted wrote:

> A park is a work of art, designed to produce certain effects upon the mind of men. There should be nothing in it[,] absolutely nothing—not a foot of surface nor a spear of grass—which does not represent study, design, a sagacious consideration & application of known laws of cause & effect with reference to that end.

Nature follows divine knowledge, and art follows nature, said Dante Alighieri in the *Commedia*. This park is art or it is landscape art, but it is more compelling than what existed in its place. Olmsted and Vaux imposed a civilizing urban plan on marshy fields to make Brooklyn a more coherent city. I did not realize back then that the horse was guaranteed to fall because Brooklyn was destined to become a metropolis.

After five years, I am still trying to figure out what this horse means to me, and I don't think it is just a coincidence connected to the photograph of my friend surrounded by horses in a field. The horse is scenery: majestic, outsize, an anachronism. I observe horses with more attention now. They are worth studying—for their contours and for their personalities. As far back as the Ice Age, people studied wild horses and understood their mien, says Wendy Williams in her fascinating *The Horse: An Epic History of Our Noble Companion*. I collected facts. Most horses are between 1.4 and 1.8 meters tall at the withers, where the neck meets the back, and weigh between 300 and 1,000 kilograms. They have two front and two hind legs, and straight spines that define their contoured, ridable backs. Long, coarse manes, including forelocks between the ears, cascade down a horse's neck and stop at the withers. The tail is part of the horse's spinal column, and has fifteen to eighteen vertebrae that decrease in size toward the tip, and those joints make it easy for horses to swing the tail fast and swat away flies and insects. The coarsest hair on the body grows on the tail, and like human hair, horsehair is made of keratin, a protein. Domesticated horses live between twenty-five and thirty years. The workhorses of nineteenth-century New York City died after two years. It is better to be one of the last horses in Brooklyn than to be part of the economy of the nineteenth century.

Williams is better than me at seeing beyond the facts. "We see horses standing in our barns and pastures and mistakenly assume that what we see is the essence of 'horse,'" she says. A horse's skeleton resembles our own, but the pieces are put together differently. We share a four-million-year history. The horse's ancestors were alive fifty-six million years ago, and he endured "tens of millions of years of global heat spikes, fluctuating ice ages, tectonic upheavals, volcanic mega-explosions, and many other planetary forces until, today, he has mastered the art of adjusting."

Humans are also good at adjusting to their circumstances. All those months I was walking in the park, I took photographs of tree branches weighted with snow, and found the fence that backed up to the local zoo to steal a glimpse of the peacock lounging. On television, we watched cities lock down while elephants and flamingoes ventured into the streets, and then we talked about it on social media. New York City social life revolved around neighborhoods, the way the urban planner Jane Jacobs believed they should. It happened in an instant.

We supported our communities by volunteering at food banks, delivering groceries to elderly people, and ordering takeout to support restaurants, and we exercised, socialized, and ate in our yards. People stayed out later with their children and made fires at the grills that the Parks Department had installed for dinner once they realized that all winter, people had been making small bonfires already. We felt less deranged in the park. Just as Olmsted and Vaux intended, the scenery worked unconsciously to influence us.

But there is a secret history. J. S. T. Stranahan—the accoladed parks commissioner known for his work as a supporter and steward of open space in Brooklyn—must have known about, or had a hand in, an 1862 report that makes clear that 1861, one year after the Civil War broke out, was a convenient time to identify properties on the site, offer payments to landlords, and, reported the sleuthing poet Marianne Moore, quietly remove the "shanties and their squatter tenants."

In 1865, while the country was still immersed in and distracted by the Civil War, Stranahan (who got his start as a developer), made his case, in the Annual Report of the Commissioners of Prospect Park, to "quietly" clear the area designated for development:

> A considerable portion of the park property is found to be encumbered with small—many of them dilapidated—buildings, which the Board has concluded to sell. But there are several good dwelling-houses, which may be advantageously rented until the ground on which they stand may be required for the purposes of improvement. Among the small houses referred to, quite a large number are occupied by mere trespassers on the land, who are being quietly removed, and very soon the entire premises will have been cleared of all objectionable features and fully prepared for the entrance of the landscape gardener.

This is the entirety of the archives about the shanties or squatter tenants. I don't know the exact location of the homes that were displaced, but I know that Park Slope got a good deal. With wide, tree-lined streets, and mansions and carriage houses fronting the park, Park Slope is one of the most beautiful towns in New York City. People here are rich, healthy, and for a time when their children are young, they are in love.

We are stewards of what happens to us, so when I walk on the public pleasure ground that Olmsted and Vaux built, I feel the violence of what men did to the land, and the pleasure of what the land does for me. It is simultaneously artificial and wild, and with years of planning and excavation work—and the removal of "objectionable features"—wilderness grew in the swampland of nineteenth-century Brooklyn. We are all immigrants and squatters in America. It is part of my social contract to preserve memories. For the record: Tinkerbell, the horse that fell, is a sturdy chestnut-copper older horse with a white face and underbelly, and gray fluffs of meringue on her ankles. I know how precisely it resembles egg whites baked at 450 degrees on top of a base of lemon because my mother's grand achievement was a lemon meringue pie that clearly had love in it because I feel it even now, though she has been dead for more than twenty years and her love for me was always a little burned.

That evening, after we saw the horse fall on the road and exit the park on shaky legs, we kept walking—but while I wept, I felt so cared for by all the trees looming over me like nurses in the dark. These were the trees that Olmsted planted. Beveridge (the editor of Olmsted's papers) said he believed that for Olmsted, scenery worked on us unconsciously, and it resembled music in that it was about thought and not words.

(Wilhelm Kempff is playing the second movement of Beethoven's Sonata 3 in C Major, with that appoggiatura uplifting on the beat as if gently reminding me that my friend's life is ending with beautiful clarity, for she is in love with the history of her life full of love and her good luck to have had three sons and a boyfriend and his family who loved her, and me.)

The path ahead was difficult to navigate and there was nothing to say so we did not talk. I could barely see where my feet were going—but I believe that what I don't see will always help me discover what by accident I stumble across. I heard the rustle of dead leaves that smelled like jaggery, and felt the ground soften under my feet. I held Jerry's arm and wondered how many thousands of cries these old-growth trees had absorbed in their bark. Their spindly fingers rose up to heaven with our great grief, so much are the gifts of love and consolation on this Earth.

It didn't take long for cancer to weaken my friend. Within weeks of her diagnosis, she became too tired to hold her phone up, so her sons held it for her when she had the energy to talk. They shared the notes and photographs she received from friends, family, and me. I sent her a photograph of an antique-style gas lamp on a path to the Long Meadow at twilight, and a dramatic shot of a spooky pond in which a craggy dead trunk is dramatically reflected. Life felt unorchestrated then, and although the scene looked wild, Olmsted and Vaux had created that reflection. Even in an abyss, a reflection is a memory. I took a photo of two flowers in bloom on a sheet of glass at a stained glass store, and sent her that, too. All of life is artificial.

I wondered about the photograph of Fiona with the horses. I'd always assumed that it was taken in Edinburgh, a moody place where horses roam the countryside between castles and ruins. I emailed this question to her middle son. He wrote back with her explanation: the photo was taken in Princetown, New York. She had been afraid of horses, but that changed after she hugged one. She and her then-boyfriend slept in the field with the horses that night. I slept in a field with her youngest son when I was nineteen. We spread our sleeping bags on a hill in the Upper Hudson. It was snowing and we had no tent. I worried that we would freeze, but he said the sleeping bag would protect me from freezing as long as it didn't dip below five degrees.

My friend became ashes in the Rockies. What Olmsted and Vaux wanted was for us to feel that all the elements of the park were harmonious, and they wanted us to keep us walking. They designed a restorative experience that would be a memory and a solace, and they gave us plenty of space to design our own experiences. You cannot escape death in the park because there are benches and trees commemorating those we loved; it is everywhere, it is in the Quaker Cemetery and in pop-up memorials and in the dead branches of the dead trees, and the seasons, and this, too, is harmonious.

Fiona Burde in Princetown, New York.

Epiphany at the 'Y'

LEARNING TO SWIM LATER IN LIFE

I ended up at the YMCA as a last resort. Years of chronic neck and back spasms had stolen all the variety and fun I used to find in working out, especially that amped-up endorphin high. By my early fifties, I'd spent thousands of dollars trying to mitigate this pain with alternative treatments after burning through one routine after another: running, kickboxing, spinning, kung fu, weight training, aerobics, Zumba, walking, children's karate, and Feldenkrais. And yet knots clung to my spine like barnacles and flared up after such innocuous activities as doing the dishes or just sitting funny.

Once strong enough to propel me through the air in handsprings, sprint down a track, and dodge oncoming players in rugby, my muscles had begun to atrophy by age thirty. A physical therapist told me then that it is not uncommon for dancers or gymnasts to remain hyperflexible as they age, but the brain thinks something is amiss when there's too much rubbery movement, and so it orders everything into lockdown. It's the brain's way of keeping you safe even though you feel horribly unsafe because your body is in spasm. I haven't been able to do a sit-up for decades, since the year my mother died, one year before I got pregnant. That was twenty-four years ago.

The maladies of age begin long before white hair and a declining physique greet you across the dividing line of fifty. When you reach menopause, you meet your new body. Mine was less peppy than before and more unpredictable. It had absorbed the shock of getting divorced and made me a cliché of a woman in her forties. At fifty, migraines pursued me daily. Medication to stave them off shaved twenty pounds from my thin frame. I seized up at the tiniest events. Neuromas in both feet stung like electric shocks when they got inflamed and made weight-bearing exercise impossible. I traded down kickboxing and spin for the elliptical and the recumbent exercise bike, but I was barely moving on those machines—never broke a sweat, never got stronger, only got more depressed. I gave up the gym, the outdoors. I decided to try swimming.

Swimming was low-impact cardio that would pump my heart as it downshifted into middle age. It would supposedly make me fit, alert, even-keeled, strong-minded, and noble. And on the way to the YMCA's big, new, shiny pool, I'd see sunshine. My mood would improve.

On my first day of this new me, I bought an elastic pink cap emblazoned with the YMCA logo from the lady at the desk and trudged down the rubber-coated stairs in my favorite peacock-print bathing suit, quietly appalled at the bacteria smearing themselves onto my feet. I pushed open the door to the swimming pool with a towel. Two lithely sculpted lifeguards tallied the activity from tall white chairs that flanked either side of the pool. People were here to learn, to improve, to disappear into the anonymizing water as they escaped the chaos of their homes and the unpredictable city streets. Things happened in quiet, slight resistance: water has a buoying immediacy and responds to every minor adjustment you make as you flip-flap down the lane. As time and laps accumulate, you hope it will pay off.

Being stuck with swimming instead of land exercise was my worst-case scenario. I grew up taking lessons year-round at Bombay's exclusive Breach Candy swimming club, next to the Arabian Sea—a privileged place where you were expected to succeed—and still more lessons at the community pool in New Jersey, but never got the hang of freestyle. I could hold my breath for a long time underwater, but I couldn't time my breathing properly while thrashing; I always ended up guzzling water and standing up instead of treading water. Swimmers, I decided, were elite people. I was just an ordinary girl who had nightmares about drowning.

And here I was, with this momentous feeling. I gazed at the pool and told myself to get in fast or I'd never do it. I hung up my towel, crouched over the lane, and threw myself in.

On my first lap, swimming breaststroke in the slow lane, an older woman touched my foot as she passed. When she tapped and paddled around me a second time, I stood up in the water and yelled: "What are you doing? Stop touching my foot!" No peace in the pool: I shared the slow lane with animosity. I was there for fitness and the good life. I did not want this woman to interfere with my effort to follow the rules, which already seemed restrictive because they required me to swim to the deep end and back without pause and without veering into or kicking others in the same lane. I didn't know how to adjust my speed to accommodate faster swimmers. I didn't know that standing politely outside the pool would seldom get a swimmer to stop and agree whether we should circle together or split the lane. Most serious swimmers would do flip turns endlessly, never really surfacing, to buy themselves more solo time. I learned to get into the water, position myself in the center of the lane, and block someone's path if I wanted to get their attention. That was the way to secure my right to swim. How was I supposed to understand the psychology of the lap lane? I thought it was about swimming. But what is swimming about? It was as if all the aggressions and disappointments that happen outside the pool followed you into it. At first, all I wanted to do was propel myself through the water without anxiety. Slowly, I wanted to feel like I could handle myself. Eventually, I wanted to be excited to be there.

I observed other swimmers intensely, memorizing their moves, admiring their technique, and probably seemed a little creepy. Instead of dreading the hard slap of cold water, I let it flow over me and refused to tense my shoulders. I told myself that, like ice, the water would help prevent migraines. When I pushed off the edge, I said to myself, *blue*, like a mantra key to the sublime. My mind emptied when I was submerged. Time was blue. My old friend, Fiona, who died, was blue, and every day she met me there underwater. Thinking got left behind in a blur as I entered the thrill of that quiet blue world.

The swimming pool at the Y reminded me of the impossibly clear and utterly freezing Lake Wolfgang, in the Austrian Lake District, where a straw-haired woman in her sixties who was swimming in lazy circles tried to entice me in. "The water is so clean you can drink it!" she said, and then she drank it, laughing. Above the steeples and terraced timber houses around the lake rose the low green peaks of the Salzkammergut range. The storybook setting made me wonder if the odds of living a peaceful life are greater where a lake is the centerpiece of a community. The personality of the village shifted according to the rhythms of precipitation and temperature rather than to the beat of the interior life. If I went back to such a place, I would not be circumscribed by anything, not even my own abilities. Getting older wouldn't be so bad with the shimmer of the lake to vivify me.

Continually in play were the colors of emerald, lapis, and opal on the water's surface, and purple shadows climbing down the hills at dusk. The air was cool enough for a jacket and gloves, and I shivered at the thought of jumping in. The woman swam backward, paddling happily while talking to me and my then toddler on the pier. She was on the far side of life and fully alert to pleasure. She had settled into a routine in which the temperature did not disrupt her swim. She was outdoors under alpine light, and maybe the plunge made her gasp, but it strengthened her lungs each time she sank in. "Come in," she said. "You will never see anything like this again." That true statement still rings in my ears.

It would have been so easy to run back to my hotel, slip on my bathing suit, and wade in. I will always regret that I had not been more daring. What I remember most was how she moved through the water without design, sweeping forward in a breaststroke that slowed into a lackadaisical sidestroke, paddling backward as she laughed, swimming in one direction, then drifting in another.

I have thought about that woman for fifteen years. I know that lap swimming in an indoor pool should make me hardier, and is something to be proud of as it builds confidence and strength, but it will never invite me to choreograph the gestures of being out in the wild under big skies.

The closest I came to swimming with any kind of freedom happened in those first weeks at the Y, when I defaulted to the sidestroke. I turned on my back and paddled with a mellow attitude. It wasn't a bad option because it afforded me a view through the skylights that ran the entire length of the soaring room. As I shimmied down the lane, leaves, robins, clouds, sky, smoke, and a red church entered and exited the panels, one after another, and made it feel a little like being outdoors.

To be honest, though, the sidestroke is a plodding repetition. This minimum-wage task of swimming brought memories of my mother ailing along without the determination of freestylers in the lanes at the community pool in New Jersey. Sidestroke is the bane of middle age, the worry you'll become so limited that you cannot adjust to the multiple simultaneous demands not only of staying afloat but also of advancing with skills you earn, and which give you a more complex experience. You will never get to the end of the pool, you will never get to the end of the person you are becoming in and outside the pool, you will never become as wise as you once were strong. The more laps you accumulate over the years, as muscle shrinks and skin loosens and breaths get shorter, the more you will have to rely on the ability to make adjustments.

You cannot straighten out your life by swimming between two lines, but you can discover a few things: you can control your stroke better if you slow down, and the patience and endurance you acquire inside the pool follow you outside. Eventually, you improve.

The YMCA has always been a symbol of resilience and renewal. It began as a faith-led organization and expanded over time to accommodate young men's varied needs and keep them off the street. The Prospect Park Y opened in 1927 in a six-story building with a neo-Georgian design on Ninth Street. It sported a grand lobby, blue leather furniture, and wood paneling. There were open fireplaces, a billiards room adjacent to the gym, a soda fountain, a tailor, phone booths, dining rooms, a "boys' division" designed to resemble an Adirondack cabin, a swimming pool, and residences for 260 men.

The new lap pool at the Y opened in 2014. The original 1927 swimming pool must have looked good once, but when my son took lessons, it was a small, dank pool in a claustrophobic room with low ceilings. I sat with other moms on plastic seats behind a painted brick divider and clapped while his lips turned blue. It must feel magnificent, even heroic, to be young, to hold on to the edge while kicking and splashing and hearing the giant ruckus you create with other children. You catch your mother's eye. She claps at all you can do, and screams "Great job!" All her cheers are for you.

It is easy to think, when you are young, that you will become some kind of hero. You will excel at whatever it is you love, and maybe you will make lots of money or win great prizes. After plenty of love affairs, you will marry a good-looking partner and grow old together in your good life. But what exactly is a good life? When you fail, do you know what you have failed at? Swimming? Love? "Experience is never limited, and it is never complete," said Henry James. Try to swim or try to love and you have succeeded already.

When I was fit, I would look in the mirror and think I was young—long after I actually was. I looked and felt the same, but of course I wasn't. Time crawled, and then suddenly sped up, and the illusion of feeling young was over.

I chose to swim because it was a way to escape or reimagine my circumstances. I've always dreaded a fate akin to the fictional character Millicent Kramer, the elderly woman in Philip Roth's *Everyman* who suffers from searing back pain. "Don't accord it power. Don't cooperate with it," she says of her condition, which she tried to mitigate with three back surgeries. "I repeat this to myself a million times a day . . . and then suddenly it's so awful I have to lie down on the floor in the middle of the supermarket and all the words are meaningless." She kills herself ten days later, a coda to the story of a miserably ordinary age-torn life. I want to believe that normalcy includes an existence free of suffering. If I cannot make myself whole, I am ruined.

I was so terrified of being infirm and hopeless, like Millicent, that I did not think twice about getting into the water on the day I saw a sign warning swimmers that the lap pool had a dangerously low temperature. I'd missed my chance in Austria, and I didn't want to get in the habit of missing chances when conditions weren't ideal. Swimming daily was my ritual and I didn't want to skip it.

Something about the regularity made it seem like things could be managed if not fixed there. Maybe the swimmers at the Y had discovered that in the process of removing their clothes, emptying their minds, and cycling through strokes, they could pump and crawl through the psychic pain that inevitably arrives, and know that creaky bones, weak lungs, and tight lats hinder but do not ruin the experience.

History is filled with heroes who are swimmers, Karen Eva Carr reminds us, in her *Shifting Currents: A World History of Swimming*. When Homer's Odysseus leaves his lover Calypso to continue his journey home to Ithaca, Poseidon creates an onslaught of crashing waves and stormy weather, yet, with the help of other gods, Odysseus dives, drifts, and survives. Julius Caesar was a great swimmer. The poorly behaved Romantic poet Lord Byron, who had a clubfoot, thrived in the water, and even swam across the Hellespont. For Plato, not knowing how to swim was a metaphor for being stupid.

Benjamin Franklin was a different kind of hero. In his 1747 pamphlet *Proposals relating to the Education of Youth in Pennsylvania*, he believed an "academy" should be set up for boarding scholars to study arithmetic, geometry, astronomy, handwriting, drawing, grammar and style, oratory, and history—and, for the sake of their health, their exercise should include running, leaping, wrestling, and swimming. Franklin set up his academy. It graduated the first college class in 1757, and merged with the state university to become the University of Pennsylvania in 1791.

A liberal arts education was always supposed to be about learning how to handle yourself. My son's college still holds fast to a 1905 requirement that students know how to swim. (Only seven colleges in the United States still require students to pass a swim test in order to graduate.) Before starting freshman year, my son had to swim seventy-five yards without stopping. I did not think he could do it. The university considers it a life skill to break the cycle of non-swimmer parents whose fear discourages their children from learning to swim and puts those children at risk of drowning. Besides the service academies (military schools), my son's college was first in the country to require a swim test.

What kind of education was I giving myself? What life skills was I gaining? Why couldn't I be a swimmer and a hero? I went into the pool and swam my eight or ten laps, figuring I could get used to the cold and build up to longer distances, and maybe one day it wouldn't make me hurt like hell and I would get better at it.

But if I got used to being hopeless, that too would be failure. To swim was to resist an ending in which I could not find relief. Move forward! Flap around a little! I hated the idea of swimming as a last resort. Then I berated myself for having nothing more enthusiastic to tell myself. I started talking to the women I saw in the locker room, and hanging out a little longer. Sometimes I went in the sauna. The woman who touched my foot that first day in the pool usually took the locker next to mine, and we became friendly. She told me stories about her dog, her trips upstate, her grandchildren. I asked people in the pool how long they'd been swimming, and explained how I was teaching myself to swim. They offered tips, encouragement. One woman swam by my side so I could match my strokes to hers. Someone else offered to imitate how I was swimming, so I could see what I was doing wrong. It turned out that even the most elite swimmers had aches, soreness, disillusion. Everyone had bad days, but they kept swimming.

I've been telling you a story of myself as a witless and spastic swimmer, but I was making it across the lanes one way or another. I adjusted my strokes. Repeat, repeat, repeat! Go home, use Biofreeze, take Advil, sit against the heating pad. Unless you think it is only valuable to be in the first five decades of your life, there is everything to look forward to.

"Swim with the swimmers, wrestle with the wrestlers, march in line with the firemen, and pause, listen, count," Walt Whitman said. The fantasy of Whitman's America turns on the feeling of renewal we are all entitled to, no matter our skills and what we think we are capable of doing. In America, in the Brooklyn that started as farmland and was radically transformed into one of the most artsy, individualistic, and sought-after places to live, all you have to do is show up and remember that no one is better equipped to experience life than you.

One day, I joined the lane of a woman who moved slowly, performing handstands, cartwheels, ballet steps. She submerged herself before exploding out of the water, arms up, a 1950s girl in a cake. She was taking forever to move down the slow lane. She was having a grand time. I watched her with dismay for five minutes. When the acrobatics girl finally did a spin, she saw me waiting. I waved. She waved back, indicating now she would swim. Suddenly it didn't matter how long she took. The spirited way she entranced herself with her practice reminded me how many ways there are, even when you are roped in, to make yourself free.

I showed up at the YMCA every day, inserted myself in the pool, and pretended that I was not freezing. Months passed. Besides my twelve minutes in the pool, my days were dreary. I lived for my mornings. I pushed off, kept my shoulders down while repeating the word blue and told myself this was my destiny. This was my destiny! Other swimmers dolphin-swam or flip-turned for what seemed to be an eternity. I counted laps while others counted miles. No one smiled or frowned. They precision-tuned their days by moving their limbs in ways that felt physically meaningful, and that would save them from sadness, obesity, affliction, injury, early death. Cardio would give them half of what they needed; toning would give them the rest. Fitness makes you more resilient to a world that attacks you every which way after you leave the ruler-straight safety of the indoor pool.

One morning, I decided that if it took me thirty years, goddamn water, I'd do it, I'd learn to swim freestyle, and if I died trying, that would be something in itself. I'd dedicate a half-lap to freestyle after every swim, from that day to forever. I pushed off, moving fast and without thinking, moving everything at once—arms like wheels one after another, legs scissoring, and my breath at the center of my body. I completed a set of strokes and began another. I had done it, I was swimming freestyle. Shocked, I stopped swimming, waded to the front of the pool, hoisted myself up, and left.

I returned the next day, stared at the lane, got in, pushed off. My gears worked it out and I swam a lap. At the far end of the lane, hyperventilating, I folded my arms over the edge and started to laugh.

I got out of the pool grinning. After three months of swimming daily, I had figured out freestyle. Swimming isn't something you can be taught just by following the rules. You have to figure out how to move intuitively, and you have to want it. Middle age isn't something you can prepare for adequately. You have to figure out how to move through it intuitively, and you have to endure it.

The calculated, rhythmic motions of doing sidestrokes and breaststrokes over time had trained me to make adjustments naturally as I swam. The repetition had taught my shopworn, atrophied, spasm-prone limbs to move in unison. Gone was the safe edge of the pool, gone were my worries, gone was the hustle of looking for happiness and managing my life, and gone was the disappointment of everything I couldn't do.

My son is making his way through college, figuring out what he is good at and how the world responds to him. The time of caring for a child and preparing him to be independent is over—replaced by learning how to support him from afar, and never with enough information. Love is no longer intuitive or easy. Like swimming, you earn it through time, emptying the dishwasher, folding laundry, shopping for groceries, talking about books, arguing about the apocalypse, and accompanying one another to gloomy procedures or parties. You adjust the way you talk to one another, and you adjust the quality of love you accept and the shape of the love you offer next. You take your giant calcium pills and lower your intake of wine, sugar, salt, dairy, and carbs, and increase your intake of steps, friends, and vegetables. You bulk up if you are thin, lose weight if you are fat. You tell yourself you can learn new things.

After fourteen months of swimming, my imperative strokes chopped up the soft blue water. My feet fluttered on the surface, my brain orchestrated the rest. Stretch the arm forward. Downsweep, insweep, backsweep. Rotate the hip, turn the face, inhale above water, exhale underwater. Repeat, repeat, repeat. I switched from the slow lane to the slow-medium lane and thought: My postmenopausal physique is not so bad after all.

My swimming wasn't particularly skillful, but it was good enough. Too often, my right, enthusiastic arm stretched straight up without bending the elbow, and my left, sluggish arm barely scaled the surface of the water. I forgot to kick my legs, and zigzagged or sank before remembering to kick my legs again.

I sometimes wondered how I'd manage if swimming were taken away, if it just ended. There was so much happening to me: invisible physics, the dance of love, the energy of waves, attention to order, the engine of the human system, the light of age, the long arms of experience, the realization that everyone was vulnerable. I fell in love with the woman who cartwheeled down the lane, the stalwart silver-haired man who strode in with deliberation, the older lady who gravitated forward like a Galapagos turtle, the other older woman with scoliosis and dynamite pump-iron legs that propelled her through fifty fast laps, and the svelte triathlete who looked like Michael Phelps and told me he didn't start swimming until his twenties because his professional-swimmer parents refused to let him join the swim team when he was younger to save him the misery of competing.

Every day of those months, I looked forward to seeing them. I slipped on my swim-skin, flung my torso forward in my usual style, and, before coming alive, for one paradisiacal moment, I sank. The water smacked my shoulders and I slipped the temperature on like a silk dress in the half-light of one day merging with the next, without landmarks or a landscape for reference. By now I'm in the middle of the lane, pressing forward. There is a sea change in my body.

My shoulders tighten in the evening. My shoulders loosen in the morning. For those twelve minutes, the blue world is impossibly clear, and my pain is gone.

Killing a Bat

I'd always been a killer, but I didn't know it until a bat flew into the castle where I was living in Italy. It was nine o'clock in the evening. I was settling in after a meaty dinner and writing a poem when a shadow interrupted me.

The bat ricocheted around so fast that I could track only its shadow on the walls. I worried that its intrusion would ruin my evening, my poem, my concentration, my well-being. My first thought was to narrow the space it could inhabit. I ducked and ran across the main room and closed the door to the bedroom. Safe inside the bedroom were my cool, airtight dreams, which arrived when I locked the shutters each night. I closed the glass windows, then the shutters, and slid bolts into barrels to keep the outside world from blowing the windows open. The castle cradled me in darkness to protect me, but I wonder if the only thing I needed protection from was myself. Dragonflies and birds greeted me in dialect from the hedge when I opened the shutters in the morning.

The castle changed the feeling of the air itself. The stones smelled like old maps and lime, and they possessed countless stories of people's lives and the lives that their imaginations created. People left but their stories lingered. My room was on the third floor, just past a torso made of sliced-up strips of aluminum cans. The man who made the torso had one story about why he chose those materials and what he discovered in Italy, and the torso had another story that began when its maker left the castle and returned home. The torso with the Italian birthright hung on a hook above a mahogany dresser, glittering in the artificial light of the hallway. It was a reminder that we interpret what feels human in ways that make sense to us, and in those supernatural feelings, something dazzling stirs to life.

The castle was everything the universe outside was not. For six weeks, fourteen artists and I captured the sun, collected the colors of the clouds, and stuffed our observations and feelings in our pockets so we could use them later in our work. We ate what arrived from the sky, sprung from the ground, and fell from the vines. In the library, writers collected armloads of books, composers rummaged for scores, and artists flipped through monographs. We were looking for ideas, colors, or sounds to lift from books or from the landscape.

The bat had flown into my room from the window that faced east. The castle sat on a steep hill, and converted horse stables that resembled giant arms reached out from the castle walls and met at the front gate, which was always locked except for an hour on laundry days. Beyond the castle walls, cypress trees guarded the road. There were no locks on doors inside the castle apartments or on the grounds. To lock the doors would mean that we were locking everything else out—including the trust that would encourage us to share conversation and let in viscous or dreamy thoughts. Anyone could open your door—but no one would. We never worried about being interrupted. The project of the castle was to remove all physical obstacles that lock you into prior or rigid ways of thinking. You could infer, from this approach, that your risks were not outside the door but interior.

It is difficult to be an artist. By the time you write something down, the paper is no longer the same paper it was seconds earlier. Sentences are full of promise and mistakes, and hours feel lousy until you settle into a rhythm in which the world seems to lack circumference—so when the practice you spent so much time cultivating is threatened, it can destroy your sense of being an artist. This is why, as an artist, you have to be relentless about removing obstacles.

The bat-shadow angled up the wall and swung up onto the ceiling. The bat perched in the rafters. I closed the door to the bathroom, which gazed at me with the excitement of a serial killer. Like the bedroom, the bathroom had personality. Daily, it acted out a surreal drama, as if warning me not to fall for appearances. The appliances looked beautiful, but they were unruly. Water pooled mysteriously around the claw tooth tub, so I was always stepping out of rain showers on my shoulders into forced baptisms at my ankles. Perhaps I had not taken myself seriously enough. The castle came after you if you did not do what was necessary to be an artist. The showerhead misbehaved: it flung itself off the metal hook and fire-hosed the turreted room. Barbarian appliances, polished and machined to appear contemporary, got restless easily, and I never knew how the room would behave.

I closed the door that led to the bedroom and bathroom. I told myself that the bat was not interested in me and would echolocate its way out. Twenty minutes passed while I flattened my body against the wall or ducked when it flapped and torpedoed toward me, swung up to the rafters again, and scissored across the room during its descent.

The bat wheeled around in a rising chorus of itself, and hovered at the height of the curve it graphed. It whipped back so fast you'd have thought my room was an inversion, outside and not inside, in the wild instead of protected from the wild. This was a place of manicured lawns and lush evergreen English laurel hedges that marked the borders between you and the feral, uncultivated world. Below the lower hedges, in a kind of queen's bench, was an herb garden, lemon trees, entire urns scented with flowering stalks of rosemary, and the most presumptuous wild roses ever to flip-flap their petals in the prime of life on an estate in Italy.

Voices cheered the match on from pages in my room. Writers and their characters yelled at me all day long already—stacks of paperbacks and hardcovers crushed one another to reach the top position where they would seduce me. "Pick me up! Turn my pages!" I'd organized the books according to what was new to me and intrigued me most, but old hats Geoffrey Hill and John Ashbery kept making their way to the top. So I dug deeper into Hill's "Apology for the Revival of Christian Architecture in England," again, its vertical style emblematic of the intellectually striving British character. He was not apologizing, and he seemed a little impatient. It wasn't a real apology for imperialism. We never really apologize for what we intend to do. It was the triumph of the British character over sky, God, technology—and an embrace of ambition that created the conditions for the British to be so noble that they would see promise and conquer it. Spires punctured and goaded the weathered sky, and still they kept building. I wanted to dislike and dismiss his explanation, but I believed him. The British had imagined they could colonize and inhabit the geography of the sky with vertical architecture—and expansion by sea. What would I do in order to expand the geography of my mind? It is human nature to want something so intensely that you would savage and rule whomever you encountered to get it.

As an artist, every day is a moral dilemma or a reckoning, but if you interrogate your thinking, it is possible to make the spaces you do not understand more meaningful. An Icelandic composer who I met in Italy told me that the long, barely occupied silences in his concerto did not eschew traditional melody but expanded it. I had misunderstood his intention, the first time I listened to his music. Melodies existed in the composer's piece, but they were so stretched out over time that I couldn't hear them. The torso hanging in the hallway, which I passed several times a day with increasing admiration, had something to say about becoming a whole person—about loving the shiny torso that hung there instead of filling in arms and legs that were implied, as if that would make the torso whole. In order to become an artist you have to understand how to become a whole person without being complete.

Every morning I foraged for words from books and examined the ways that other poets hitched couplets together or turned an idea on a syllable or an em dash. I was myself but not myself. I chased disorganizing and disruptive turns of phrases just off the beat. The noise of hesitations, with their ricocheting sound waves, offered a musical challenge: Should I wait for the diminuendo into silence or speak? Composers train their ears for years, learning to orchestrate for instruments they don't play, so I have to ask myself, when I write, whether an oboe and a forklift together make a sound that resonates, and whether I am making noise or music.

I breathed in sentences from other writers: Eavan Boland, Thom

Gunn, and Ciaran Carson were left of my computer until Michael Palmer's *Letters to Zanzotto* became first violin. Montale read me his *Xenia* poems in the chair while his dead wife Mosca waltzed above the pages. Zanzotto's fat green book bent my mind; I wondered if I could right-turn my approach to mirror his agile and maniac but not illogical style. If I could see the concepts inside the green front cover, as if I were not Zanzotto but his mind at work (if I could be the torso), maybe then I could follow the physics of his poems. In Jean Follain's prose poems, a character on the page held up a mirror and brushed her thick flaxen hair. In "Hammerfest," Auden arrived aglow in Sweden, pleased that he could fall into festival days properly; he didn't speak the language, so his ears could use their lifelong training to really hear. Cesare Pavese matchboxed his memory of bonfires, Ashbery his "Instruction Manual," and Antonio Tabucchi the omelet-eating Pereira, a journalist who plays it safe under the Salazar dictatorship until he meets a young leftist for whom he commits one courageous act. I think we act with courage when we care about one other. For example, it is Virgil, not Beatrice, for whom Dante Alighieri keeps going. Every evening, I looked over my day's work.

I texted the group of artists on WhatsApp: "Who knows how to make a bat leave the room?" A composer sent an emoji. "Can someone help me?" I asked. A petite painter with an earnest spirit showed up with a towel, snapping the fabric at the bat to shoo it away. The bat perched on a rafter and folded its wings around itself. Something is always out of reach. The woman suggested turning off the lights; it would fly out eventually. I looked at her in horror. It would chew my eyes out when I opened the door to use the bathroom. She asked her husband F to come while I texted the group again and requested a tall man.

If I were more noble, I'd welcome the bat into my life as a good luck charm instead of as a threat. Bats are the only flying mammals on Earth. They eat 1,200 mosquitoes an hour. They are just like me, all over the place and determined to cause havoc, steal nectar, and haunt humans by diving at them in the dark.

The bat seemed to want to stay with me. My room was a coliseum and the last fight of the day was the bat and me. I cursed my windows, which had no screens. Bees circled around the overhead light all day while I worked at my desk, their monotonic buzzing a counterpoint to the lyrical ways I wanted my sentences to unfold. They didn't bother me, and maybe I was secretly proud that the element of danger they added had not distracted me. If I was gambling with the bees, it was out of necessity, but it was also true that the allegory of coexisting with these stinging insects was the story of allowing a little danger in my home in order to get more serendipity. If I did not fear getting stung, I probably would not get stung. But there was no way to apply this mindset to the bat, because it was a giant hurtling threat—and if bats preferred darkness over light, and my room was well lit, clearly something was wrong with my world or something was wrong with it.

Several people wrote with suggestions: open the window, turn off the lights, leave the room. By then three tall men and the petite painter milled about, craning their necks to understand the bat's situation and figure out what to do next. The bat seemed small, and I wanted to believe that it was innocuous, but bats seem as if they are waiting to attach themselves to my skin like an IV line and drink my blood. In the same way, a trainer-entertainer in a cage with a lion at a circus whips the ground near the lion to demonstrate to the audience how violent it is. The lion cues up and issues a terrible roar. Then, just to show you that nature cannot be tamed, and animals do not love you, the lion opens its giant maw and digs its teeth into the trainer, who loses blood while men with whips leap in to attend to the beast's ordinary behavior.

This is surely the sound that prefigures the Second Coming and the process of becoming whatever our soul and body stitch together at the end (or the beginning) of eternity. It is the violent roar of feeling between entry and exit; the door is unlocked and it opens from every direction. The door is in the middle of the room. You are in the middle of orchestrating a symphony or glazing a sculpture or recombining the sentences in a poem that you have reworked so many times that it is crying.

The tallest man in the group looked at me with a sweet, earnest face and lowered his voice. "There's something wrong with it. It's a baby. It's not going to leave. Do you want me to kill it?"

I put my face in my hands in horror and embarrassment, and nodded. It was the quickest solution. I ran out of my room and into the kitchen and closed the door. Banging, silence. I returned with a broom and dustpan, feeling squeamish and sheepish. I did not offer to remove the bat, but handed the dustpan to the men, who threw the baby bat in the trash, and then I methodically cleaned up the scene of the crime, which only took five minutes. I cursed the window, bolted it shut, and sat down in my chair to work.

Acknowledgments

Portions of this book have first appeared in the following publications: AGNI, *Virginia Quarterly Review*, the *Paris Review Daily*, *Southern Humanities Review*, *The Common*, *American Literary Review*, Longreads, *Harvard Divinity Bulletin*, the *Kenyon Review*, and *Air/Light*.

Many thanks to the incredible team at the University of Georgia Press and to my editors Bethany Snead and Nicole Walker for believing in this book. I've been lucky to have fabulous editors: Paul Reyes, Sari Botton, Wendy McDowell, Elliott Holt, Nicole Terez Dutton, David Ulin, Justin Gardiner, Emily Everett, Bill Pierce, Jill Talbot, and Sadie Stein. I could not have written this book without the input and support of my aunt Bharati Sanghvi and my father, Dilip Mehta. Friends and family read drafts, offered advice and edits, and cheered me on: Nina Mehta, James Marcus, Ivan Russell, Jerry Sticker, Tom Russell, Minna Zallman Proctor, Edwin Frank, Garnette Cadogan, Chris Hallman, Cliff Thompson, Yxta Murray, Sven Birkerts, Alexander Chee, Vivian Gornick, Askold Melnyczuk, Catherine Parnell, Katie Freeman, Adrian Frazier, Jordan Smith, Frances Marie-Uitti, Mary Carlson, and Dana Prescott. Special thanks to Timofei Babenko for translating the Dostoevsky epigraph from *The Idiot*.

The Café Royal Cultural Foundation gave me a generous grant to support work on this collection, and Rosemarie Heinegg supported my work with the Union College Peter Heinegg Foundation grant, in honor of her husband and my former English professor. Grazie molto to Civitella Ranieri, Yaddo, and the Virginia Center for the Creative Arts for time and space to write. Love to Mike Mewshaw and Linda Mewshaw for sponsoring my time at Civitella and offering unconditional and lifelong friendship, mentorship, and pasta. Thank you to my neurologist Myrna Cardiel for saving me from a life of daily migraines.

CRUX, THE GEORGIA SERIES IN LITERARY NONFICTION

Debra Monroe, *My Unsentimental Education*
Sonja Livingston, *Ladies Night at the Dreamland*
Jericho Parms, *Lost Wax: Essays*
Priscilla Long, *Fire and Stone: Where Do We Come From? What Are We? Where Are We Going?*
Sarah Gorham, *Alpine Apprentice*
Tracy Daugherty, *Let Us Build Us a City*
Brian Doyle, *Hoop: A Basketball Life in Ninety-Five Essays*
Michael Martone, *Brooding: Arias, Choruses, Lullabies, Follies, Dirges, and a Duet*
Andrew Menard, *Learning from Thoreau*
Dustin Parsons, *Exploded View: Essays on Fatherhood, with Diagrams*
Clinton Crockett Peters, *Pandora's Garden: Kudzu, Cockroaches, and Other Misfits of Ecology*
André Joseph Gallant, *A High Low Tide: The Revival of a Southern Oyster*
Justin Gardiner, *Beneath the Shadow: Legacy and Longing in the Antarctic*
Emily Arnason Casey, *Made Holy: Essays*
Sejal Shah, *This Is One Way to Dance: Essays*
Lee Gutkind, *My Last Eight Thousand Days: An American Male in His Seventies*
Cecile Pineda, *Entry without Inspection: A Writer's Life in El Norte*
Anjali Enjeti, *Southbound: Essays on Identity, Inheritance, and Social Change*
Clinton Crockett Peters, *Mountain Madness: Found and Lost in the Peaks of America and Japan*
Steve Majors, *High Yella: A Modern Family Memoir*

Julia Ridley Smith, *The Sum of Trifles*
Siân Griffiths, *The Sum of Her Parts: Essays*
Ned Stuckey-French, *One by One, the Stars: Essays*
John Griswold, *The Age of Clear Profit: Collected Essays on Home and the Narrow Road*
Joseph Geha, *Kitchen Arabic: How My Family Came to America and the Recipes We Brought with Us*
Lawrence Lenhart, *Backvalley Ferrets: A Rewilding of the Colorado Plateau*
Sarah Beth Childers, *Prodigals: A Sister's Memoir of Appalachia*
Jodi Varon, *Your Eyes Will Be My Window: Essays*
Sandra Gail Lambert, *My Withered Legs and Other Essays*
Brooke Champagne, *Nola Face*
Diane Mehta, *Happier Far: Essays*